"Cheryl Betz is a devoted student and teacher of the Scriptures whom God has gifted in the writing of *Lord, It's Time for Just You and Me* (Volumes I, II, and III) to help us experience the joy and peace that comes from devotional and mediation time with God."

—Bill Baird, III, Elder, First Presbyterian Church, Pikeville, Kentucky

"I was gifted Cheryl's first devotional *Lord, It's Time for Just You and Me*. Her stories, choice of Scriptures, and prayers have had such a positive impact on my life. I have since bought her second devotional and have been able to share it with others. Her words and stories have made it easier to help make Godly decisions that we all wrestle with as young wives and mothers. God has used her to be a blessing to all who read her wonderful book."

—Allison Cooper, young wife and mother

"The everyday ups and downs of life can be difficult to handle. *Lord, It's Time for Just You and Me* is kept within my arm's reach daily. The relatable stories, Scripture readings, and prayers so often give me what I need to have a Christ-centered day. It's a blessing in my life."

—Linda Lepore, Retired Director of Development of a Non-Profit Company

"I believe this book is an invitation to develop an open, candid, and honest relationship with your best friend—Jesus. You are invited into His presence in a similar way Cheryl uses to introduce and engage friends with one another—engaging, warm, honest, and loving. You will see Cheryl and Jesus together in a friendship that will draw you to Him in a remarkable and intimate way."

—Rosemary W. Lukens, RN, MA, Moderator, Evangelical Presbyterian Church

"When I pick up this sweet devotional *Lord, It's Time for Just You and Me*, the title itself sets the stage for focus on God and reminds me to let the competing intrusions of life fade into the background. Cheryl speaks with great insight and simplicity as she shares personal stories through which she's learned Biblical truths. I'm looking forward to more touching tales from the wellspring of her life experiences."

—Robyn Phillips-Madson, DO, MPH FACOFP
Founding Dean (retired) and Professor of Family Medicine and Public Health
University of the Incarnate Word School of Osteopathic Medicine

"Cheryl writes this devotional in down-to-earth, easy-to-understand language that inspires her readers to want to live the way the Lord wants us to live. Her use of Scripture makes it relevant to our lives in a fresh way. *Lord, It's Time for Just You and Me* was a blessing to read."

—Judi Patton, former First Lady of Kentucky

"Cheryl Betz's devotionals have been an inspiration to me. Her eloquent way of delivering a Scripture passage, a practical way to live out that passage in my daily life, and a plan of action have led me closer to my relationship with the Holy Spirit. They have helped push me further in my spiritual journey. I highly recommend her devotionals as support in your growth as you walk with Christ."

—Mary Reilly, Cheryl's sister in Christ

BOOK 3

Lord, IT'S TIME FOR JUST *You* AND *Me*

A DEVOTIONAL BY

Cheryl Lynn Betz

LUCIDBOOKS

Lord, It's Time for Just You and Me, Book 3
A Devotional
Copyright © 2023 by Cheryl Lynn Betz

Published by Lucid Books in Houston, TX
www.LucidBooks.com

All rights reserved. No part of this publication may be reproduced, stored in a retrieval system, or transmitted in any form by any means, electronic, mechanical, photocopy, recording, or otherwise, without the prior permission of the publisher or Cheryl Lynn Betz, except as provided for by USA copyright law.

All Scripture quotations, unless otherwise indicated, are taken from The Holy Bible, New International Version®, NIV®. Copyright ©1973, 1978, 1984, 2011 by Biblica, Inc.™ Used by permission of Zondervan. All rights reserved worldwide. www.zondervan.com The "NIV" and "New International Version" are trademarks registered in the United States Patent and Trademark Office by Biblica, Inc.™

Scripture quotations marked (ESV) are taken from the ESV® Bible (The Holy Bible, English Standard Version®), copyright © 2001 by Crossway, a publishing ministry of Good News Publishers. Used by permission. All rights reserved.

Scripture quotations marked (NASB) are taken from the (NASB®) New American Standard Bible®, Copyright © 1960, 1971, 1977, 1995, 2020 by The Lockman Foundation. Used by permission. All rights reserved. www.lockman.org

Scripture quotations marked (NKJV) are taken from the New King James Version®. Copyright © 1982 by Thomas Nelson. Used by permission. All rights reserved.

Scripture quotations marked (NLT) are taken from the Holy Bible, New Living Translation, copyright ©1996, 2004, 2015 by Tyndale House Foundation. Used by permission of Tyndale House Publishers, Carol Stream, Illinois 60188. All rights reserved.

Scripture quotations marked (RSV) are taken from The Revised Standard Version of the Bible, copyright © 1946, Old Testament section copyright © 1952 by the Division of Christian Education of the National Council of the Churches of Christ in the United States of America and are used by permission. All rights reserved

Scripture quotations marked (TLB) are taken from The Living Bible copyright © 1971. Used by permission of Tyndale House Publishers, a Division of Tyndale House Ministries, Carol Stream, Illinois 60188. All rights reserved.

Scripture quotations marked MSG are taken from THE MESSAGE, copyright © 1993, 2002, 2018 by Eugene H. Peterson. Used by permission of NavPress. All rights reserved. Represented by Tyndale House Publishers, a Division of Tyndale House Ministries.

eISBN: 978-1-63296-611-7
ISBN: 978-1-63296-610-0

Special Sales: Most Lucid Books titles are available in special quantity discounts. Custom imprinting or excerpting can also be done to fit special needs. Contact Lucid Books at Info@LucidBooks.com

This book is dedicated to my Lord, my family, and all of my readers and beloved sisters- and brothers-in-Christ who love me, flawed that I am. I love you and thank God for you.

SPECIAL THANKS

No person can accomplish any work entirely on her own, and I am no exception. There are many people who have contributed to getting this work to this point, and I am grateful and thank God for each one.

First, I am grateful for my family: my husband, William T. Betz, D.O., who has not only fixed many dinners while I have been focused on writing but has supported me with each of my books. I thank God for our adult children: our daughter and son-in-law, Amy and Brian Casselberry; our son and daughter-in-law, the Reverend John M. Betz and Kristi Betz, M.D. PhD. They tolerated my endless questions and requests for help as I wrote *Lord, It's Time for Just You and Me, Book 3*.

Next, I want to thank the many pastors who have served and are serving our Lord and from whose instruction I have benefitted significantly. I thank the Lord for Dr. Trent Casto, the Reverend Chris Voorhees, the Reverend Aaron Dean, the Reverend Bradley C. Smart, the Reverend Alistair Begg, and the late Reverend Charles Ashmore. Praise God for pastors who preach God's Word boldly and without apology.

I also want to thank my precious friend Vicki Jubanowsky for encouraging me greatly in my writing even to the point of helping me edit some of my works. Mary Reilly is another of my dear friends who continues to bless my socks off as she praises my work to other people. I want to add many thanks to my friend Pam Guilander and her daughter, Allison Guilander Cooper, who have opened the door for the Holy Spirit to use my work to bless their friends. There is a wonderful group of women who have prayed for me and encouraged me through the writing and publishing process. These precious sisters-in-Christ are Carol Anderson, Barb Domino, Gail Hanson, Vicki Jubanowsky, Cathy Miserendino, Alyce Reck, Karen Sainato, Cindy Schmidler, and Lee Stuckey. What a blessing all of these women are! All praise to God for giving me such extraordinary friends.

In addition, I want to thank the team at Lucid Book Publishing for their encouragement, their attention to detail, and their professional approach to publishing. I am grateful to have worked with them.

Even in naming all of these people, I am sure there are those whom I have failed to name. I am so very grateful for the fact that as believers we are all part of Christ's body and that we serve Him together as He directs us (1 Corinthians 12:4-27).

Finally, let me conclude with this: I have no authority but that which the Lord has given me. I have no gifts but those which He has bestowed upon me. I have no life but that which He has breathed into me. And of course, I have no words but those which He has created. Thank You, Lord, for these gifts, and please, Lord, breathe life into these words to Your glory.

TABLE OF CONTENTS

  Letter to the Reader   xvii

  Suggestions in Using this Devotional   xix

1. **Admittance**   1
   a. Scripture Reading: John 10:7-18
   b. Scripture Quoted: John 10:9
   c. Theme: We can get to heaven by Christ alone.

2. **Adventures**   5
   a. Scripture Reading: Psalm 139:1-18
   b. Scripture Quoted: Psalm 119:96-97
   c. Theme: Reading the Bible is an adventure.

3. **Ants**   9
   a. Scripture Reading: Psalm 1:1-3 and 119:9-18
   b. Scripture Quoted: Ecclesiastes 3:1
   c. Theme: Guard your quiet time with the Lord.

4. **Aunt Merle**   11
   a. Scripture Reading: Luke 9:46-48 and 1 Peter 4:8-11
   b. Scriptures Quoted: Mark 12:31 and John 13:34
   c. Theme: Love your neighbor.

5. **The Blind Man**   13
   a. Scripture Reading: Luke 18:35-43
   b. Scriptures Quoted: Luke 18:38
   c. Theme: We need to have eyes to see Jesus and what He is doing.

6. **Boasting**   15
   a. Scripture Reading: Deuteronomy 6:10-12
   b. Scriptures Quoted: Jeremiah 9:23-24
   c. Theme: Our boast should be about our Lord.

7. **The Breeze**   17
   a. Scripture Reading: John 14:15-31
   b. Scriptures Quoted: John 14:26
   c. Theme: We are blessed to have the "breeze" of the Holy Spirit who lives in us and teaches us what we need to know.

8. **But God**   19
   a. Scripture Reading: Philippians 4:4-8
   b. Scripture Quoted: Philippians 4:19
   c. Theme: God is in control of our lives.

9. **Butterflies and Other Personalities**   21
   a. Scripture Reading: John 15:1-8
   b. Scripture Quoted: Galatians 5:22-23
   c. Theme: Be the person God created you to be.

10. **Change of Leadership**   25
    a. Scripture Reading: Titus 3:1-2
    b. Scripture Quoted: Psalm 75:6
    c. Theme: Pray for the new leader.

11. **Chosen**   27
    a. Scripture Reading: Ephesians 1:1-14
    b. Scripture Quoted: Ephesians 1:4-5
    c. Theme: God chose us before the creation of the world.

12. **Coincidence**   29
    a. Scripture Reading: Acts 10-11:35
    b. Scripture Quoted: Isaiah 46:9-11
    c. Theme: There are no coincidences for the Christian.

13. **Comfortable**   33
    a. Scripture Reading: Acts 10:9-16
    b. Scripture Quoted: Philippians 4:11b
    c. Theme: God's plan for our lives may not always be in our comfort zone.

14. **Confirm Your Facts**   37
    a. Scripture Reading: Luke 7:11-28
    b. Scripture Quoted: Luke 7:18-19
    c. Theme: Each person needs to confirm for him or herself that Christ is the Messiah.

15. **Depart, Depart**   41
    a. Scripture Reading: Psalm 143
    b. Scripture Quoted: Psalm 32:8
    c. Theme: God loves for us to pray for specific needs.

16. **Division in the Body**   45
    a. Scripture Reading: 1 Corinthians 12:12-27
    b. Scriptures Quoted: 1 Corinthians 12:25-26 and Galatians 5:25-26
    c. Theme: All churches should live in harmony with one another.

17. **Entertaining Strangers**   49
   a. Scripture Reading: Acts 2:42-47
   b. Scripture Quoted: Hebrews 13:1-2
   c. Theme: Our Lord expects us to include strangers when we entertain.

18. **Fear Not**   51
   a. Scripture Reading: Genesis 3
   b. Scriptures Quoted: Genesis 2:16-17
   c. Theme: We are not to fear and we are to avoid exposure to evil.

19. **GPS (Global Positioning System)**   55
   a. Scripture Reading: Exodus 13:1-18
   b. Scripture Quoted: Exodus 13:17
   c. Theme: God's directions are perfect.

20. **Glorify God**   57
   a. Scripture Reading: Psalm 16:5-11
   b. Scripture Quoted: 1 Corinthians 10:31
   c. Theme: All that we do is for God's glory not for our glory.

21. **God's Guidance**   59
   a. Scripture Reading: Psalm 121
   b. Scriptures Quoted: Psalm 32:8 and Matthew 7:7-8
   c. Theme: God wants us to ask Him for guidance.

22. **God's Work in Us**   63
   a. Scripture Reading: Romans 8:28-30
   b. Scriptures Quoted: 2 Corinthians 3:18 and Ephesians 2:10
   c. Theme: God is supernaturally changing us to be more like Christ.

23. **The Good Samaritan**   67
   a. Scripture Reading: Luke 10:25-37
   b. Scriptures Quoted: Luke 10:33
   c. Theme: Our neighbor is anyone in need.

24. **The Good Shepherd**   69
   a. Scripture Reading: John 10:1-30
   b. Scripture Quoted: John 10:11
   c. Theme: The shepherds were blessed to witness the Good Shepherd.

25. **Grace Extenders**   71
   a. Scripture Reading: Psalm 100
   b. Scripture Quoted: Ephesians 2:8-9
   c. Theme: We should all be grace extenders.

26. **Group Dynamics**   73
    a. Scripture Reading: 2 Corinthians 5:17-21
    b. Scripture Quoted: 2 Corinthians 2:15-16
    c. Theme: We are Christ's Ambassadors no matter which group we are in.

27. **Have You Told Anyone Lately?**   77
    a. Scripture Reading: Luke 8:26-39
    b. Scripture Quoted: Luke 8:38-39
    c. Theme: Tell people what God has done for you.

28. **His Love Endures Forever**   79
    a. Scripture Reading: Psalm 136
    b. Scripture Quoted: Isaiah 54:10
    c. Theme: God's love for us endures/lasts forever.

29. **His Sovereignty**   81
    a. Scripture Reading: Psalm 71
    b. Scripture Quoted: Psalm 71:17
    c. Theme: God is our Sovereign who guides our lives.

30. **Invisible**   85
    a. Scripture Reading: 1 Samuel 3:1-10
    b. Scripture Quoted: 1 Thessalonians 5:16-18
    c. Theme: God is always with us and listens when we pray.

31. **Just Turn the Page!**   87
    a. Scripture Reading: Acts 10:9-16
    b. Scripture Quoted: 2 Timothy 3:16-17
    c. Theme: You cannot escape when God's Word is convicting you.

32. **Leaders**   91
    a. Scripture Reading: 1 Kings 1:1-53
    b. Scriptures Quoted: Proverbs 19:21 and Romans 13:1
    c. Theme: God chooses our leaders.

33. **Let Us Be Salty Salt and Shining Lights**   93
    a. Scripture Reading: Psalm 19
    b. Scriptures Quoted: Matthew 5:13-16
    c. Theme: As we live our day-to-day lives, we need to be salt and light to the world.

34. **Misplaced Expectations**   97
    a. Scripture Reading: Ephesians 2:1-10
    b. Scriptures Quoted: Matthew 7:7-8
    c. Theme: Test your expectations to be sure they are correctly placed.

35. **Nehemiah—Part 1—Fasts and Prays**   101
   a. Scripture Reading: Nehemiah 1-2:8
   b. Scriptures Quoted: Nehemiah 2:5
   c. Theme: When approaching a problem, fast, pray, prepare, and present.

36. **Nehemiah—Part 2—Experiences Opposition**   105
   a. Scripture Reading: Nehemiah 2:8-20
   b. Scriptures Quoted: Proverb 21:1
   c. Theme: Don't let yourself become distracted or discouraged when obeying God's call on your life.

37. **Nehemiah—Part 3—Prepares and Presents**   107
   a. Scripture Reading: Nehemiah 2:11-18
   b. Scriptures Quoted: Nehemiah 2:17b
   c. Theme: Do your homework and use discernment in disclosing your plans.

38. **Nehemiah—Part 4—His Work is Challenged**   109
   a. Scripture Reading: Nehemiah 2:19-20; 4:1-23; 6:1-4, 15-16
   b. Scriptures Quoted: Nehemiah 6:16
   c. Theme: Stay focused on completing God's assignment and ask God for discernment as problems arise.

39. **Our Home Churches**   113
   a. Scripture Reading: Romans 12:3-16
   b. Scriptures Quoted: Psalm 119:105, John 13:34, and Matthew 7:7-8
   c. Theme: God has a church for all of us.

40. **Our Place in Heaven**   117
   a. Scripture Reading: John 14:1-4
   b. Scriptures Quoted: John 14:2
   c. Theme: Jesus is preparing a place for us in heaven.

41. **Our Speech**   119
   a. Scripture Reading: Ephesians 5:1-17
   b. Scriptures Quoted: Ephesians 5:4
   c. Theme: As Christians our speech should glorify God.

42. **Parents' Love for Their Children**   123
   a. Scripture Reading: Psalm 139:1-18
   b. Scriptures Quoted: Psalm 127:3
   c. Theme: Parents should not show favor of one child over another.

43. **Persecution**   125
    a. Scripture Reading: Matthew 5:10-12
    b. Scriptures Quoted: Matthew 5:10
    c. Theme: If you are being persecuted, be sure it is because you are standing in Christ and not because you are behaving badly.

44. **Plans**   129
    a. Scripture Reading: Psalm 23
    b. Scriptures Quoted: Proverb 16:1
    c. Theme: Make plans that can be altered by God.

45. **Praise the Lord**   131
    a. Scripture Reading: Psalm 148
    b. Scriptures Quoted: Psalm 145:9-10a
    c. Theme: All God created can, does, and will praise Him.

46. **Prayers**   133
    a. Scripture Reading: Matthew 7:7-11
    b. Scriptures Quoted: Ephesians 3:20-21
    c. Theme: Our Heavenly Father wants to give us good gifts.

47. **Pride and Humility**   137
    a. Scripture Reading: Philippians 2:5-8
    b. Scriptures Quoted: Philippians 2:8
    c. Theme: God wants us to be humble.

48. **Reflect Him**   139
    a. Scripture Reading: Exodus 34:29-35
    b. Scriptures Quoted: 2 Corinthians 3:18
    c. Theme: We are to reflect our Lord.

49. **Remembering**   141
    a. Scripture Reading: Deuteronomy 8:1-18
    b. Scriptures Quoted: 1 Corinthians 11:23b-25
    c. Theme: God is big on remembering.

50. **Righteous**   143
    a. Scripture Reading: 1 John 1:7-10
    b. Scriptures Quoted: 1 John 1:9
    c. Theme: We are righteous only in and because of Christ.

51. **The "Right" Way**   147
    a. Scripture Reading: Philippians 2:3-11
    b. Scripture Quoted: Philippians 2:14-15
    c. Theme: Take on humility; cast off arrogance.

52. **Say "Thank You"**   149
   a. Scripture Reading: Luke 17:11-19
   b. Scriptures Quoted: Colossians 3:17 and 1 Thessalonians 5:11
   c. Theme: We must remember to thank God and people.

53. **Simeon**   153
   a. Scripture Reading: Luke 2:21-35
   b. Scriptures Quoted: Luke 2:29-32
   c. Theme: As God continued to encourage Simeon, Joseph, and Mary, He will continue to encourage us.

54. **Sitting on the Outside, but Dancing on the Inside**   155
   a. Scripture Reading: Psalm 150
   b. Scripture Quoted: Psalm 149:3
   c. Theme: Praise the Lord with our whole being.

55. **Souvenirs**   157
   a. Scripture Reading: Ecclesiastes 4:9-12 and 1 Peter 4:8-10
   b. Scriptures Quoted: Colossians 1:16
   c. Theme: God blesses us with friends from different countries.

56. **A Sure Foundation**   161
   a. Scripture Reading: Matthew 7:24-27
   b. Scripture Quoted: Matthew 7:24
   c. Theme: Our lives need to be built on Christ, our sure foundation.

57. **Take the Headlines to the Prayer Closet**   163
   a. Scripture Reading: Luke 11:9-13
   b. Scripture Quoted: Philippians 4:6 and 1 Timothy 2:1
   c. Theme: Pray for those we see in the media.

58. **Trees**   165
   a. Scripture Reading: Psalm 139:1-18
   b. Scripture Quoted: Matthew 5:13-14
   c. Theme: Thank God that He created you just the way you are.

59. **Uncomfortable**   167
   a. Scripture Reading: Exodus 20:1-17
   b. Scripture Quoted: 2 Timothy 2:15-16
   c. Theme: Sometimes preaching God's Word makes us uncomfortable.

60. **Zacchaeus**   171
   a. Scripture Reading: Luke 19:1-10
   b. Scripture Quoted: Luke 19:5
   c. Theme: Jesus seeks out His loved ones.

Appendix I—Salvation Scriptures and 3 Questions to
        Ask When Introducing Someone to Christ   173

Appendix II—Step-by-Step Scriptures   175

Appendix III—Scriptures Used in this Devotional and
Listed in Biblical Order   181

One Last Note from the Author   189

LETTER TO THE READER

Thank you so very much for choosing this devotional! To those of you who have read my first and second books, *Lord, It's Time for Just You and Me* and *Lord, It's Time for Just You and Me, Book 2,* you will see that I have kept the same general layout in Book 3 that I have in my first two books. The content of this new book includes different stories and principles from those in *Books 1* and *2*. I pray that you will use it as a method to draw closer to the Lord. I also pray that you grow in your faith and that He uses this offering to draw you closer to Him.

At the beginning of each devotional reading, I have given two Scripture references. One is a brief verse or two printed at the top of the page for those frantic, on-the-run mornings, and the other gives the reference for a longer reading, which you can do when you have the time. God's Word is life and will give you so much more than any devotional filled with a man's or woman's words. How grateful I am that we have so many Bible translations available to us! I have found that a diet of reading His Word satisfies me as nothing else can.

Whether you are a new or mature Christian, I pray that the Holy Spirit will minister to you with His Word as you proceed through this devotional. I pray that as you spend time with Him, you will be blessed and become progressively more and more like Christ until you meet Him face to face. Let this be a time when you can sit before the Lord and say, "Lord, it's time for just You and me. Speak, for Your servant hears."

Enjoy and accept God's many blessings!

Blessed in His service and His love,
Cheryl Lynn Betz, a fellow work-in-progress

SUGGESTIONS FOR USING THIS DEVOTIONAL

Please allow me to offer a few suggestions that might enable you to glean optimal benefit as you use this book:

- **Block off a time each day** when you can sit before the Lord and say, "Okay, Lord, this is our time. It's just You and me."
- **Pray each day before you begin to read.** Ask the Lord for a fresh word for the day. I love Psalm 119:18 from *The Living Bible*: **"Open my eyes to see wonderful things in your Word."** This is my prayer for you. May the time you spend in this book and reading the Bible be profitable for the kingdom because it is time spent with our Lord.
- **Listen and believe.** Expect the Lord to speak to you today. Expect the message to be pertinent to your life. Look for His direction, encouragement, instruction, and answers in the Scriptures and accompanying message provided in each reading. If you see no current relevance of them to your life, ask Him to reveal His message throughout the day. The author of the Book of Hebrews makes an important observation in verse 2 of chapter 4: "For we also have had the gospel preached to us, just as they did; but the message they heard was of no value to them, because those who heard did not combine it with faith." I pray that as you read this book and God's Word you will "combine it with faith."
- **Use a Bible that you can understand** as you read the **Scripture Reading** at the beginning of each day. This book is a devotional, not a Bible study. Its function is to encourage you to spend time everyday in fellowship with our Lord and enhance the time you spend with Him. If you are struggling with a version of the Bible that is hard to understand, your focus will be on the words rather than on the meaning. If the Bible is new to you, I recommend using the New Living Translation, the New International Version, or The

New English Version. These are reliable translations that are easier to understand than some of the other versions.

- This devotional is not a substitute for Bible study. I highly recommend that you **seek out a Bible study in your church where you can study God's Word in depth.** Usually there are several Bible studies offered in a church. Even in our small 350-member church in Kentucky, we offered several Bible studies: one during the Sunday school hour for adults, one during the week for men, another for women, and one for teens. Look for a study that teaches the Bible from a spiritual rather than an academic view. Principally, the emphasis should be: What is the Lord saying in the Scriptures for us today? What are the principles He wants me to learn, and how can I put them into practice? What are His promises on which I can stand in my everyday life?
- **This book is written by a human being, not God.** Therefore, it is possible that I have made mistakes. However, I have gone to great lengths to be sure of the accuracy of what I have written. I pray I have handled His Word correctly according to 2 Timothy 2:15.
- **Keep a devotional journal** where you can list the date of your specific prayer requests and leave space for the date upon which you receive an answer. This is also a good place to note specific, time-pertinent messages you receive from the Lord. You can keep track of questions that you have asked the Lord, such as, "Are You telling me to quit my job and move, or is this a diversion from the enemy?" Every time you believe He is talking to you about an issue, you can jot it down under your question.
- You will notice that in **Appendix II** I have listed several Scriptures that pertain to the way the Lord faithfully leads us, step by step, showing us which way to go and how we can rely on Him to help us grow toward spiritual maturity. You may want to refer to these Scriptures on those days when your spiritual progress seems slow and you need some encouragement.

Let me send you forward with a promise from His Word and then a blessing. First, the promise is from Philippians 1:6: "I am certain that God, who began the good work within you, will continue his work until it is finally finished on the day when Christ Jesus returns" (NLT). Next is the blessing from Hebrews 13:20-21:

> "May the God of peace, who through the blood of the eternal covenant brought back from the dead our Lord Jesus, that great Shepherd of the sheep, equip you with everything good for doing his will, and may he work in us what is pleasing to him, through Jesus Christ, to whom be glory for ever and ever. Amen."

ADMITTANCE

Scripture Reading: John 10:7-18

"I am the gate; whoever enters through me will be saved" (John 10:9).

On my way to Bible study, I received a call from our Bible study leader. Because there was an accident in front of the main entrance to our development, she couldn't get in through the front gate, and as you have probably guessed, our Bible study is in a gated community. Most of the new developments in southwest Florida are gated. There are only two ways to get in. One is through the front gate and the other is through the back gate. In order for visitors to come in, they have to stop at the front gate where an attendant checks to make sure they are on the list of invited people. Only residents of the development have transponders on their cars to let them in the back gate. Consequently, I met her outside the development; she got in my car, and since my car has a transponder, we were able to get into the community through the back gate.

This made me think about the similarity between entrance into our community and entrance to heaven. With our community, guests can only enter through the front gate. With heaven people can only get in one way, and that is with Jesus. He said, "I am the way and the truth and the life. No one comes to the Father except through me" (John 14:6). He also said, "I am the gate, whoever enters through me will be saved" (John 10:9). Jesus is our "transponder" or key to open the door of heaven to us.

Although I could bring in our Bible study leader by having her in my car, that doesn't work with entrance to heaven. As much as I would like to bring others in with me when I go, I cannot. Every person is admitted or denied entrance solely on his/her decision to accept or reject Christ's sacrifice on his/her behalf. Do they believe that Jesus sacrificed Himself for their sins and then was raised to life in three days? We know that over five hundred people were blessed to actually see Him alive after having been crucified and dead in a tomb.

Have you ever shared your faith with anyone? Perhaps you are afraid you won't do a good job. The amazing thing is that if you have an opportunity to speak with someone about your relationship with the Lord, He will guide you through the conversation. It's always good to use Scripture as you relay your experience. You know that God's Word is never wasted (Isaiah 55:11). I have some Scriptures in Appendix 1 at the back of this book that you may want to use, or you may have some that are especially meaningful from the time you accepted Christ as your Savior.

It's also good to do a bit of preparation to be ready if God gives you an opening. Keep in mind that God wants you—and all of us believers—to share your faith. It's His idea. "Go into all the world and preach the gospel to all creation" (Mark 16:15).

Plan of Action:

1. It would probably increase your confidence in sharing your faith if you did a bit of preparation. One of the Bible studies I have done suggested that you begin with "Before I trusted Christ . . . " Write down what you were like before you became a Christian. Follow that with "How I trusted Christ . . . " How did you become a Christian? Finally, write down "Since I have trusted Christ . . . " Make note of how you have changed since you became a Christian. Don't make any of your answers too long, and don't over dramatize or glamorize about how bad you were before Christ. You don't want to put the focus on that rather than on how graciously God received you into His family.

2. Ask God to give you an opportunity to share your faith. Then be ready because He will, and it will bless your socks off!

Prayer:

Father, please give us wisdom and discipline to be ready to share our faith with anyone You place in our path. It is a very serious, life-and-death opportunity, and we don't want to miss it. Love people through me. Instill in me a sensitivity that can tell when someone is ready to hear Your words. Your kindness leads us to repent. Help me to exhibit kindness in a way that You are pleased. I am Yours. I put my life in Your hands now and in the future. I want to follow You and obey Your leading. Thank You, Lord, for revealing Yourself to me. I know others whom I pray will come to know You and accept Your Son as their Savior. Help me to be ready, Lord, for any opportunity You place before me. I pray in Jesus' name. Amen.

ADVENTURES

Scripture Reading: Psalm 139:1-18

"Nothing is perfect except your words. Oh, how I love them. I think about them all day long" (Psalm 119:96-97 TLB).

When I was a little girl, we lived by a forest where I would explore with the kids in the neighborhood. We walked the paths between the trees with the anticipation of finding some treasure. Sometimes the grass was high, and we were eaten up by chiggers; but that was the price we were willing to pay for the adventure. I have to admit that even now when I walk by the preserve area in our development, and I see the paths that go through them, my inner child is tempted to follow them to see what treasure I might find.

As an adult, I do feel that same sense of adventure in the morning when I get ready to read the Scripture for the day. Since God's Word is living (Hebrews 4:12), it is new every morning, and we can expect to find something special just for us from Him as we read His Word. Often I begin with this Scripture as my prayer: "Open my eyes to see wonderful things in your Word" (Psalm 119:18 TLB). It's not uncommon for me to read more than the set Scripture listed in the guide that I usually follow. I get so interested in what God is saying that I read on and on. I find the more I read of His Word, the more I love It and the more I love God. How blessed we are to have His written Word which we can read anytime we want.

After reading *The Hiding Place*, by Corrie Ten Boom with John and Elizabeth Sherrill, I felt God's encouragement to memorize Scripture. Although I found memorizing the French language fairly easy in high school and college, I stumbled around as I tried to memorize Scripture. I remembered that my students in French class could more easily remember the French songs than they could the dialogues they had to memorize. Therefore, I decided to ask God to give me a tune for some Scriptures that I wanted to memorize. I started with Isaiah 43:2-3a: "When you pass through the waters, I will be with you; and through the rivers, they shall not overwhelm you; when you walk through fire, you shall not be burned, and the flame shall not consume you. For I am the LORD your God" (RSV). Isn't that an awesome Scripture?! Of course, you know that God gave me a tune to sing to memorize the words. Once I had that memorized, I moved on to other Scriptures and matched tunes for them.

You see, God wants us to know His Word and have it stored in our hearts. "Let the word of Christ dwell in you richly . . . " (Colossians 3:16). We read in Psalm 119:11: "I have hidden your word in my heart that I might not sin against you." The Holy Spirit is faithful to bring Scriptures to mind as you need them (John 14:26). I remember a time when my husband was working late in the emergency room at a hospital; I had the windows open and I was doing dishes. I heard what sounded like someone walking in our yard. Immediately, the Holy Spirit reminded me of Psalm 27:2-4: "When evil men come to destroy me, they will stumble and fall! Yes, though a mighty army marches against me, my heart shall know no fear! I am confident that God will save me" (TLB). I spoke it aloud, closed the windows, and made sure the doors were locked. Yet because of God's presence and the reminder of His Word, I wasn't afraid.

2 Timothy 3:16-17 in *The Living Bible* tells us a few more wonderful reasons to read, study, and memorize the Word: "The whole Bible was given to us by inspiration from God and is useful to teach us what is true and to make us realize what is wrong in our lives; it straightens us out and helps us do what is right. It is God's way of making us well prepared at every point, fully equipped to do good to everyone."

Reading His Word takes a time commitment and discipline, but that price is worth it for an adventure where you will find treasure of eternal value.

Plan of Action:

1. As you read your Scripture reading for the day, ask God to open your eyes to see wonderful things in His Word. Then expect Him to answer your prayer because He will.

2. If you have not memorized His Word yet, consider doing so. Find a Scripture that really speaks to you, and begin work on memorizing it. You might even think about putting it to music. It worked for me.

Prayer:

Father, thank You so very much for Your Word! What a precious gift. Help me to make time every day to read it, expecting wonderful things, even adventures. And thank You for sending the Holy Spirit to teach me and then to remind me of those Scriptures when I need them. Please help me to memorize the verses that You want me to store in my heart. Thank You, Lord. I pray in Jesus' name. Amen.

ANTS

Scripture Reading: Psalm 1:1-3 and 119:9-18

"There is a time for everything, and a season for every activity under the heavens" (Ecclesiastes 3:1).

While sitting on my lanai, ready to have my quiet, seeking, learning time with my Lord, I noticed several ants busying along on my table. As I proceeded to get rid of them, I realized that I really needed to wipe down the whole tablecloth. Then I noticed that the lanai furniture needed to be cleaned. Just as I was about to start that new activity, I stopped, recognizing that I was allowing myself to be distracted from the purpose of the moment—my devotion time.

How many times are we distracted by "ants"? We are ready to be quiet and wait on the Lord, only to allow minor, insignificant distractions to interrupt our precious time with the Lord. There is no doubt that I needed to clean all of the items on my lanai. However, the timing was wrong. At that time, my devotion time needed to be my priority. I could clean the furniture when my quiet time was finished for the day.

Remember the story of Mary and Martha in Luke 10:38-42. Mary chose to sit at Jesus' feet and listen to His teaching, while Martha was "distracted by all the preparations that had to be made" (Luke 10:40). No doubt there were preparations that had to be made. That is what the Scripture says. But for that particular time when Jesus was visiting, "Mary has chosen what is better" (Luke 10:42). Let's choose what is better at the right time.

Plan of Action:

1. Ask the Lord to help you to keep your priorities in line with His.
2. Ask Him to help you to recognize when you are sidetracked by insignificant or minor distractions when you are having your quiet time with Him, and ask Him to help you stay focused on Him and His Word.

Prayer:

Lord, You know that my quiet time with You is important to me, and I know it is important to You, too. Please help me to guard our precious time together, and help me not to allow myself to be distracted. I love You Lord, and I thank You for loving me. In Jesus' name. Amen.

AUNT MERLE

Scripture Reading: Luke 9:46-48 and 1 Peter 4:8-11

"... *Love your neighbor as yourself* ..." (Mark 12:31).

"*A new command I give you: Love one another. As I have loved you, so you must love one another*" (John 13:34).

When my Aunt Merle was in her eighties, she painted her front porch steps. After they were painted, she planned to jump over the steps to the porch and go back into her home. She later told me, "You know what, Cheryl? I found out that I couldn't jump over two steps anymore!" And then she laughed and laughed. She had the best attitude. Whenever I think of her, she has that great smile on her face that crinkled up her eyes.

I heard a remarkable story about her that happened before I was born. It involved a man in our very small town who had a drinking problem and wasn't taking care of his two young children. One day, my aunt went to his house, packed up the children, and told the man that when he sobered up and could care for his children, he could come to her home and pick them up. A few days later, he sobered up and arrived at her door to bring home his children. This scenario repeated itself a few times before he sobered up for good.

I don't think we could do today what my aunt did those many years ago. But this happened in a very small town where everyone literally knew each other's business, assets, and flaws. Most of the town knew what happened, and they also knew that those children couldn't have been in better hands while they stayed with my aunt. They knew that she had not only the best interests of the children in mind, but also those of their father.

Jesus was asked by one of the religious leaders, "Of all the commandments, which is the most important?" (Mark 12:28). Jesus answered, "The most important one . . . is this: 'Hear, O Israel, the Lord our God, the Lord is one. Love the Lord your God with all your heart and with all your soul and with all your mind and with all your strength.' The second is this: 'Love your neighbor as yourself.' There is no commandment greater than these" (Mark 12:29-31). My aunt surely loved her neighbors and acted out that love for all of their safety.

When Paul wrote to Timothy about widows, he listed several activities that they were to have done before their husbands died. She " . . . is well known for her good deeds, such as bringing up children, showing hospitality, washing the feet of the saints [humbly serving other believers], helping those in trouble and devoting herself to all kinds of good deeds" (1 Timothy 5:10). This is a list that all people would do well to work toward. Aunt Merle lived that way.

Plan of Action:

1. Look for opportunities to help others.
2. Make it a habit to practice hospitality.
3. Look for ways to exhibit your love for your neighbor. When you make cookies, share them with your neighbor. When your trash has been picked up and you are bringing your empty trash bin back to your garage, move theirs close to their garage. Invite them to your home for dinner.

Prayer:

Lord, teach me to love my neighbor as You want me to. Give me eyes to see when someone needs help, and then please help me to unselfishly help them. Help me to practice hospitality. I want to live my life with a good attitude. Please teach me what I need to do that. I love You, Lord, and I am grateful that You want to help me to become more like Christ in every way. Thank You. I pray in Jesus' name. Amen.

THE BLIND MAN

Scripture Reading: Luke 18:35-43

"He called out, 'Jesus, Son of David, have mercy on me!'" (Luke 18:38).

A blind beggar, Bartimaeus (Mark 10:46), was waiting by the road hoping that someone would help him. Sadly people tended to ignore their responsibility to care for those who could not help themselves. Therefore, these helpless people were left with the only option of begging for help. Bartimaeus heard the crowd and asked what was happening. They answered that Jesus of Nazareth was passing him. He cried out "Jesus, Son of David, have mercy on me!" The Bible commentaries point out that his using the term "Son of David" signifies that he recognized Him as the long awaited Messiah. How did Bartimaeus know that Jesus was "the Son of David"? How did he recognize Jesus as the Messiah?

Although he was blind, God opened his understanding to know Jesus was the Messiah. Bartimaeus knew he was in the presence of God when Jesus passed by. Yet many of those who had the gift of vision were blind to the fact that they were walking next to the Messiah. When Bartimaeus called out, although Jesus was in the middle of a crowd, Jesus stopped and asked the man what he wanted. He replied, "Lord, I want to see" (Luke 18:41). Jesus answered, "Receive your sight; your faith has healed you" (Luke 18:42). The Bible reports that he immediately received his sight and followed Jesus, praising God. I would love to have witnessed that. What a marvelous joy he must have experienced! Luke reported that when the people around them saw what happened, they praised God too.

Just as Jesus stopped to ask Bartimaeus what he wanted Jesus to do for him, He wants to know what He can do for us. We are told over and over in God's Word that if we ask God for something in Jesus' name, He will give it to us (Matt. 7:7, 21:22; John 14:13-14, etc). Of course, we need to remember that He will not give us anything that is not good for us. He wants only the best for us, and He is really the only One who knows what is best for us. But we are also told that we have not because we ask not (James 4:2).

Bartimaeus, the blind man, knew exactly what he wanted and believed Jesus could heal him. Praise God he recognized Him as the Messiah and was bold enough to shout out and ask for help. Let's too be bold enough to ask. "In him [Jesus] and through faith in him we may approach God with freedom and confidence" (Ephesians 3:12).

Plan of Action:

1. Is there something that you want but you've been unsure whether you should pray for it? It certainly doesn't have to be something material. It may be a healing of a relationship. Whatever it is, ask the Lord. If it isn't what He sees as good for you, the answer will be no. But remember James 4:2 referred to above . . . you have not because you ask not. You can always finish your prayer with "I only want this if this is Your will for me."

2. As you go through your life, ask God to open your eyes to see Him at work. Then you can react as the crowd did around the blind man when he was healed. You can praise God for what He is doing.

Prayer:

Lord, thank You for giving Bartimaeus the gift of sight. We thank You for the many physical and mental illnesses and disabilities that You have healed. In fact, thank You for all that You do for us! Thank You even for the times when You choose not to heal or not to answer our prayers the way we want them answered because for some reason You have other plans. Lord, we trust You to give us only what is good for us. And please open our eyes to see You at work in this world. We don't want to miss Your miracles. We are grateful that You love us. In Jesus' name we pray. Amen.

BOASTING

Scripture Reading: Deuteronomy 6:10-12

"This is what the LORD says: 'Let not the wise man boast of his wisdom or the strong man boast of his strength or the rich man boast of his riches, but let him who boasts boast about this: that he understands and know me, that I am the LORD, who exercises kindness, justice and righteousness on earth, for in these I delight,' declares the LORD" (Jeremiah 9:23-24).

As Christians we know that God chose us, and we are grateful for Him beyond words. Yet we don't allow ourselves to be self-righteous, acting like we are better than others. Remember the Apostle Paul when he said, "Here is a trustworthy saying that deserves full acceptance: Christ Jesus came into the world to save sinners—of whom I am the worst" (1 Timothy 1:15). Paul wrote 13 books of the New Testament, yet he says he is the worst sinner. He also tells us to "Always be humble and gentle. Be patient with each other, making allowance for each other's faults because of your love" (Ephesians 4:2 NLT). An important characteristic that all Christians should exhibit is humility. We are saved and God does love us, but we did nothing to cause God to choose to save us. It was only by His grace upon us. "For it is by grace you have been saved, through faith—and this not from yourselves, it is a gift of God—not by works, so that no one can boast" (Ephesians 2:8-9).

Boasting about our accomplishments, our belongings, our looks, or our salvation is wrong and unattractive. Are you wealthy? Who do you suppose gave you the brains to work and gather your wealth? Who gave you the energy to complete your projects? Are you attractive? Did you combine the genes to form your body? You might want to look at Psalm 139:13: "For you [God] created my inmost being; you knit me together in my mother's womb." In this **Scripture Reading** God speaks through Moses to the Israelites warning them that when things are going well with them in the Promised Land, they might be prone to forget that the Lord provided it all. We should heed the same warning.

If we are going to boast, it should be about our amazing, wonderful, gracious God. "Therefore, as the Scriptures say, 'If you want to boast, boast only about the LORD'" (1 Corinthians 1:31 NLT). In public and in private we need to recognize that all we are and all we have has come from our God.

Plan of Action:

1. Take a few moments and thank God for all He has given you. Be specific in your thanks.
2. Now consider where He has placed you. Are you serving Him well with gratitude? Are you available to Him for service?

Prayer:

Father, please give me a grateful spirit. I know that as long as I remember all that I am and all that I have came from You, I will not tend to boast about my accomplishments or my material goods. You have been so gracious to me, and really Lord, I am grateful beyond words. I thank You for loving me and taking care of me. I thank You for giving us Your Word and for the Holy Spirit who teaches us Your truth. I am sorry that Jesus had to die for my sins; but I thank Him for opening my way to You, my heavenly Father. I love You, Lord. I pray in Jesus' name. Amen.

THE BREEZE

Scripture Reading: John 14:15-31

"But the Counselor, the Holy Spirit, whom the Father will send in my name, will teach you all things and will remind you of everything I have said to you" (John 14:26).

When my husband and I were out for a walk on a warm Florida day, the Lord sent a breeze our way. I told my husband, "Everything is better with the breeze." The Lord showed the correlation between His breezes and the Holy Spirit. Everything in the Bible is so much better because we have "the breeze" of the Holy Spirit to explain and teach us what God wants us to know. I am so grateful that Jesus told us how the Holy Spirit can help us. I am also thankful that the Father sent the Holy Spirit to live in us! We are truly blessed to have the privilege to read God's Word with the Author living inside us.

Plan of Action:

1. As you read the Bible do so knowing that God is actually speaking to you. It is His Word written to help you with life. It is personal.

2. If you have not already established a habit of setting aside a time in the day when you read His Word, you should. You will be amazed how He answers specific questions you may have. As I read the Bible, He reminds

me how His resources are unlimited and that my life is safe in His hands. He reminds me that He loves and treasures me. He encourages me to see the work He is doing in my life, and how He is changing me to look more like Christ.

Prayer:

Lord, thank You for the gentle breezes You send our way, and thank You for the breeze of the Holy Spirit. You are such a generous, loving Father. Thank You for my very life. I submit myself to You for You to work a miracle in changing me to be more like Christ. In Jesus' name I pray. Amen.

BUT GOD

Scripture Reading: Philippians 4:4-8

"And my God will meet all your needs according to the riches of his glory in Christ Jesus" (Philippians 4:19).

How many times in the Scriptures does the problem seem insurmountable, and then we read "But God..." stood between the problem and His loved one? How many times in your life have the problems seemed insurmountable, a solution impossible, but God stepped in and saved you?

I remember a time early in my husband's medical practice, I was paying bills, and I could see that we would not have enough money to cover payroll on the next day for our employees. I sat at the table in our home with our high school age daughter, and said, "We need to pray that God brings in checks tomorrow at the business to cover the amount of money I need to write in checks." So we prayed exactly that.

Of course, God brought in more than enough to cover the checks I needed to write. I remember how grateful and relieved I felt. Our daughter and I rejoiced in our wonderful God who watches over us and intervenes on our behalf more times than we have any idea. I am sure that you also can remember a time when it seemed that there was no hope, but God intervened to save your circumstance.

Plan of Action:

1. Take a few moments and think back over your life to the times when you or your situation seemed doomed, but God stepped in and saved you. An almost fatal accident? Financial ruin? You undoubtedly thanked Him at the time it happened, but it would be good to thank Him again for keeping your safe and providing for you.

2. Perhaps you've never thought of the fact that God stepped in to supply whatever you needed. Think of the barely missed car accident, that fall, that gift of food when your refrigerator was empty, or that surprise check when you had little money left. Again, think over your life, and this time, begin to make a list of how God stepped into your life and saved you.

Prayer:

Father, I am so very grateful that You are all-knowing, all-seeing, always with me, and always with my family. Thank You again for the many times You have saved our lives, literally keeping us from dying here on earth and given us new life in Jesus. We are immensely privileged to have a God, You Father, who watches over us always. Please open my eyes to see You at work in my life and in the lives of my family, friends, and neighbors. I don't want to miss any of Your work on this earth. Thank You. Thank You. Thank You. I pray in Jesus', Your precious Son's name. Amen.

"Now to him who is able to do more than all we ask or imagine, according to his power that is at work within us, to him be glory in the church and in Christ Jesus throughout all generations, for ever and ever! Amen" (Ephesians 3:20-21).

BUTTERFLIES AND OTHER PERSONALITIES

Scripture Reading: John 15:1-8

"But the fruit of the Spirit is love, joy, peace, patience, kindness, goodness, faithfulness, gentleness and self-control" (Galatians 5:22-23).

I have a friend who is like a butterfly. She moves from place to place, person to person, blessing those she is with, and providing beauty by her calm demeanor and her beautiful smile. Some people are like butterflies who leave people feeling refreshed and encouraged.

I have another friend who is like a pretty, pink, bouncing ball. She enters a room and the room lightens up. She bounces from one group to another, and each group is better because they have visited with her. She is like spring flowers brightening people's lives.

Another of my friends is like a cup of delicious, hot spiced tea. She is quite serious and introverted, and yet no less a blessing. People know that they can talk with her, and she will listen. Really listen. This even happens with people who don't know her. People who need someone to listen gravitate towards her.

Still another of my friends is like a computer, but with warmth. He is a methodical problem solver. He is quiet and introverted, but when given a problem to solve, he does so effectively and efficiently. After working with him, people are relieved and encouraged. Again, such a blessing to behold!

When I think of one of my other friends, I am reminded of a comfortable, supportive pillow. He shows as much grace to the people who have not recognized Christ as their Savior as he does to fellow Christians. He encourages them to tell him their story to which he listens intensely. He asks significant questions, and they freely answer him. In an unintimidating way, he tells them his story and shares appropriate Scriptures. When they go on their way, they do so with a few nuggets of God's Word in their minds.

Obviously these people only represent a few of my friends and their personalities. Each is a blessing in his and her own way. God made only one of each of us. We should rejoice in whom we are and allow God to bless others through us as the Holy Spirit uses our individual personalities the way He intended.

Just as I have described some of my friends, I know other people who are like big, heavy boots, stomping on all they come into contact with. They grumble and complain. They are never happy about anything and criticize everything and everyone. They leave people discouraged and anxious.

Obviously, as Christians we want to bless those with whom we come into contact. We should leave people better than we found them. How do we do that?

First, we need to draw closely to the Lord on a regular basis, and let our Lord replenish us. We cannot forever be moving around or engaged in helping others. We will run out of energy or just get burned out. We need to take time to let the Lord minister to us. If we don't, what we offer others is temporal at best. In life, we have to eat and drink to maintain our life. As Christians we need to eat and drink God's Word and take time to let Him refill us. Remember 1 Corinthians 10:31, "So whether you eat or drink or whatever you do, do it all for the glory of God." We need to submit to His washing us with His Word as is spoken of in Ephesians 5:26.

Second, we need to be sure to guard our attitude. Are we quick to criticize? Do we find ourselves grumbling? The Scripture is very plain about grumbling. Don't do it! James 5:9 states, "Don't grumble against each other, brothers, or you will be judged. The Judge is standing at the door." We are to "offer hospitality to one another without grumbling" (1 Peter 4:9). Jude uses these adjectives to describe godless men: "The men are grumblers and faultfinders; they follow their own evil desires; they boast about themselves and flatter others for their own advantage" (Jude 16).

Third, we should try to focus on the positive in each person and every situation rather than finding fault. We need to purposely look for the good in each person, and then dwell on that. If we know someone that we have trouble in seeing any good, we can ask God to open our eyes to see the good in that person. We may need to re-train ourselves by regularly speaking encouragement to ourselves and others. "Therefore encourage one another and build each other up . . . " (1 Thessalonians 5:11). Although, at first, we may feel like a hypocrite, after a time our mind will begin to absorb and believe what we are saying. Our positive speaking will literally change our mind with the help of the Holy Spirit.

Fourth, we need to make one of our life's goals to submit continually more to the working of the Holy Spirit in us by allowing Him to express kindness, goodness, and gentleness to everyone we meet and know. These are some of the fruits of the Holy Spirit that I listed at the beginning of this devotional (Galatians 5:22-23). Later in the Bible we read, "Therefore, as we have opportunity, let us do good to all people, especially to those who belong to the family of believers" (Galatians 6:10). It helps to remember Romans 12:3a where the apostle Paul instructs: "Because of the privilege and authority God has given me, I give each of you this warning: Don't think you are better than you really are" (NLT). Yes, we are sons and daughters of the King. But Christ came to the earth as a servant and told us to follow His lead and serve others as well. Also Philippians 2:3 reinforces this idea. "Do nothing out of selfish ambition or vain conceit, but in humility consider others better than yourselves." We are to love and serve others. We are to be kind, good, and gentle with others.

"But thanks be to God, who always leads us in triumphal procession in Christ and through us spreads everywhere the fragrance of the knowledge of him. For we are to God the aroma of Christ among those who are being saved and those who are perishing" (2 Corinthians 2:14-15).

Plan of Action:

1. Re-read the four suggestions I listed above, and try to put them into practice. Ask for God's help. Remember He loves to help you grow to become more like Christ.

2. Just for fun, look around at some of your friends. Whose company do you enjoy? Ask yourself why? Also look at how other people react to your friends. I believe you will observe that those who bless others draw people to them.

Prayer:

Father, thank You for the butterfly, bouncing ball, hot spiced tea, warm computer, and supportive pillow personalities whom You have placed in my life. I thank You that, like them, You made each of us unique. Because You love us just as You made us, help us to freely live in our God-given personalities. Remind us that we are to have a servant attitude in that we should always be willing to help others. Please help us to be kind, good, and gentle with everyone we meet, as well as with our friends and family. We would love to leave them better than we found them. Please let us represent You well. We are grateful that You love to help us. We truly do want to become more like Christ. In His name we pray. Amen.

CHANGE OF LEADERSHIP

Scripture Reading: Titus 3:1-2

*"For promotion and power come from nowhere on earth,
but only from God. He promotes one and deposes another"
(Psalm 75:6 TLB).*

You are working in an organization where the leader seems to fit the position perfectly. Everything flows easily. He has worn these shoes for a long time, and the leather has stretched to form-fit the position to the person and vice-versa.

One day that leader retires, and a new leader is hired. Her style of managing, her personality, and her mannerisms are different in many ways from the former leader. She wants to implement new ways of doing things that have been done the same way forever. Everything seems out of whack because there is so much change.

As a Christian, what should you do? For one thing, give her time. Just as one has to wear a new pair of shoes for a while before they become comfortable, the leader will need to work a while in the position before it becomes comfortable, and eventually, things may fall into place.

You may be tempted to grumble, complain, or gossip with other employees. Don't do it. Pray. Pray for the leader. Pray for the organization. Pray for the other employees. Pray that you will be a help and not a deterrent or hindrance. You may be called by God to be a peacemaker between the new boss and the rest of the group. "Blessed are the peacemakers, for they will be called sons of God" (Matthew 5:9). The new leader may need guidance and input from those who have occupied their positions for a while. Help as you can. Otherwise, do your job well. "Whatever you do, work at it with all your heart, as working for the Lord, not for human masters, since you know that you will receive an inheritance from the Lord as a reward. It is the Lord Christ you are serving" (Colossians 3:23-24).

A good leader builds on what the previous leader accomplished. But every person is different and may have different goals. If, after you have given the new leader time and help, you still are unhappy or uncomfortable with the leadership, you may need to ask God if that is still His place for you. Then be open to His guidance. When you ask, He will answer. Watch for His directions. He may want you to stay for a season, or He may want you to start looking for employment elsewhere.

Just remember that no job is perfect, just like no boss is perfect. In fact, no person is perfect. " . . . [F]or all have sinned and fall short of the glory of God, . . . " (Romans 3:23). As long as we are working with people, we are working with imperfect beings. With God's help, you can extend grace, and hopefully, be at peace where He has placed you. Or you may be at peace as God moves you somewhere else. Remember He wants His best for you.

Plan of Action:

1. Pray for the new leader.
2. Pray for the organization.
3. Do your best to help the new leader adjust to her job.
4. Continue to do your job to the best of your ability until the Lord directs you elsewhere.

Prayer:

Father, please give me wisdom as I deal with this new person. Guard my mouth so I won't criticize or gossip about her. If I am to help her, please give me an opening. Meanwhile, our organization needs Your help to function smoothly. Thank You, Lord. In Jesus' name. Amen.

CHOSEN

Scripture Reading: Ephesians 1:1-14

"For he chose us in him before the creation of the world to be holy and blameless in his sight. In love he predestined us to be adopted as his sons through Jesus Christ, in accordance with his pleasure and will" (Ephesians 1:4-5).

I remember when I was in the sixth grade and went to the public school. At that time in this small town, there were only two schools: the private Catholic school and the public school. I was excited because I was finally old enough to go to the dances for all of the town's sixth, seventh, and eighth graders.

At the dance, I was chatting with a group of giggly girls who had spied a very good-looking boy that we didn't recognize. Someone told us that he was an eighth grader who went to the Catholic school. I remember thinking that he could have his pick of any of the fifty girls in the building, and I privately told myself that there was absolutely no way he would look twice at me. I had no outstanding features and was a sixth grader at that. Just as this group of girls were commenting how cute he was, he looked my way and our eyes locked. He smiled, and I smiled back. He walked over to our crowd and asked if I would like to dance with him. Wow, was I surprised and very honored. It ended up that he was a very mannerly, kind young man, and that was the beginning of my first, very sweet boyfriend-girlfriend experience.

As I look back, I remember how surprised and blessed I felt that out of all the girls he could have chosen, he chose me. Do you realize that out of everyone in the world the Lord could have chosen to be His child, He chose you? Once you have accepted Christ as your Savior, He adopts you to be part of His family. It is His choice. He loves you so much that He was willing to let His Son die on the cross so you could receive His gift of eternal life. Can you grasp the fact that the God who created the universe loves you and wants you in His family? That is truly awesome.

Plan of Action:

1. Right now take time to thank God for choosing you and adopting you into His family.
2. Ask Him to help you hear Him clearly and follow His directions obediently. Accept His blessings with gratitude, and enjoy Him.

Prayer:

Father, my wonderful Father, You love me now, and You will love me forever. You have blessed me so abundantly, and I am eternally grateful. I know that by Your grace, You chose me to be Your daughter. I pray that I will always honor You in everything I do and say. Thank You, Lord. In Jesus' name. Amen.

COINCIDENCE

Scripture Reading: Acts 10-11:35

"I am God, and there is no other; I am God, and there is none like me. I make known the end from the beginning, from ancient times, what is still to come. I say, 'My purpose will stand, and I will do all that I please.' From the east I summon a bird of prey; from a far-off land, a man to fulfill my purpose. What I have said, that will I bring about; what I have planned, that will I do"
(Isaiah 46:9-11).

There are no coincidences. As we look at certain happenings in our life, we might chalk them up to coincidence. We might be surprised, but God isn't. God proclaims in His Word that He is in control of every aspect of life here on earth. God created the heavens with all their host, the earth and everything on it, and the seas and all that is in them (Nehemiah 9:6). He gives life. His power is limitless. His knowledge is limitless. God knows the number of hairs on every head (Matthew 10:30), and He knows when a sparrow falls to the ground (Matthew 10:29). Jesus makes it plain throughout His life that we are worth more than a sparrow. "You know when I sit and when I rise; you perceive my thoughts from afar. You discern my going out and my lying down; you are familiar with all my ways" (Psalm 139:2-3). We see in the verses 7-12 of Psalm 139 that there is no where that we can go where God is not there too. That is reinforced in Romans 8:38-39: "For I am convinced that neither death nor life, neither angels nor demons, neither the present nor the future, nor any powers, neither height nor depth, nor anything else in all creation, will be able to separate us from the love of God that is in Christ Jesus our Lord."

Note the **Scripture Reading** when the Lord gave Peter the vision three times of food being lowered on the sheet, and He told him to kill and eat. But Peter replied that he had never eaten such things because they were considered unclean for Jews up to this point. Then God responds, "Do not call anything impure that God has made clean" (Acts 10:15). At this time, the messengers from Cornelius showed up at the door of the home where Peter was staying.

Before Christ's life, death, and resurrection, Jews didn't meet with Gentiles. Peter said to the people in Cornelius' home, "You are well aware that it is against our law for a Jew to associate with a Gentile or visit him. But God has shown me that I should not call any man impure or unclean" (Acts 10:28). Cornelius was God fearing, but he was still a Gentile, and God planned for Peter to preach the Good News about Christ to him, his relatives, and close friends. This was a God-arranged meeting. This was the beginning of the teaching of the Gospel message to Gentiles. "This mystery is that through the gospel the Gentiles are heirs together with Israel, members together of one body, and sharers together in the promise of Christ Jesus" (Ephesians 3:6).

In Job 38-39, God is asking Job where he was while God was creating the world. This puts our lack of power and knowledge in perspective as we see just a part of what God has done and is able to do. "Where were you when I laid the earth's foundation? Who shut up the sea behind doors? Have you ever given orders to the morning?" (Job 38:4, 8, and 12). If you ever want to be reassured that you love and serve a WONDER-FULL God, just read Job 38-39.

God prepares us and equips us and provides for us always.

Plan of Action:

1. As you go through your everyday life, ask God to open your eyes to see Him at work.

2. When you look at your fellow men and women, remember what God said to Peter. He was told not to call any man impure or unclean. We leave that up to God. He created man and woman in His image. Treat your friends and neighbors as beings created by God. "Love your neighbor as yourself" (Matthew 22:39).

Prayer:

Lord, just the thought of You having everything under Your control, even my day to day life, is astounding. Your Word says that You are watching after me. How can I begin to thank You for being my God? How can I thank You for making Yourself known to me? You created everyone and all there is in the universe, and yet You are watching over me. I am in awe of You. Please help me to have a pure heart, a pure mind to follow You all day, every day. I feel so loved. Thank You, my precious God. In Jesus' name. Amen.

COMFORTABLE

Scripture Reading: Acts 10:9-16

"... for I have learned to be content whatever the circumstances"
(Philippians 4:11b).

Soon after we moved to a new community, I met someone who would become a good friend. In the process of telling each other our backgrounds, she mentioned several of the local properties which she and her husband owned. Guessing what my conclusion would be after hearing this information, she quickly added, "Oh but we're not wealthy; we're just comfortable." I am sure you have surmised with that last sentence, she meant they were financially stable enough not to have to worry about paying bills.

Since I first heard that statement, I have thought about it many times for several reasons. First of all, after I had the opportunity and time to get to know her well, I concluded that her idea of comfortable was much different than most people's. Although both she and her husband began their lives together with meager resources, after a lifetime of hard work and good investments, they were what most people would consider wealthy, despite her denial.

Another reason I have thought about her statement is because often the Lord has led me into circumstances where I have not been comfortable. I am not talking about discomfort because of a lack of resources. I am talking about times when He led us to circumstances that were totally different than we were used to. For example, in the 18th year of my husband's medical practice, He made it clear to us that we were to leave our home city where we had lived all of our lives and move to the hills of Kentucky. We loved Kansas City, our church, our friends and family, our connections, and so on. However, God confirmed to both of us in undeniable ways that He wanted us to move. We obeyed and ended up loving the mission He assigned to us. But in the beginning, we were uncomfortable. We had to make new friends, find a new church, get established in a new job, etc. Any of you who have moved know what is involved. Just the physical stress of packing is uncomfortable, yet God wanted this for us. I love what Moses said to God in Exodus 33:15, "If your Presence does not go with us, do not send us up from here." Can we all say, "Amen!" to that?

Do you think Peter was comfortable when God gave him the vision where a large sheet was put before him and on it were all kinds of animals, reptiles, and birds (Acts 10:9-16)? Then God said, "Get up, Peter, kill and eat." Peter replied, "Surely not, Lord! I have never eaten anything impure or unclean." God spoke again, "Do not call anything impure that God has made clean." This happened three times. We know that this vision prepared Peter to accept an invitation to visit the home of a Gentile. It was against the law for Jews to associate or visit a Gentile (Acts 10:28). Now, I ask again, do you think Peter was comfortable at this point? I doubt it. Yet he put aside his discomfort and followed God's guidance.

How about when Jesus confronted Paul, who was also called Saul, on the road to Damascus (Acts 9:1-10)? Do you think Paul was comfortable? Of course he wasn't. First of all, the bright light blinded him, and the men traveling with him had to lead him by the hand to Damascus. Let's look at the Christian whom God told to go meet Paul. That man was Ananias. God gave him a vision where He told him to go lay hands on Paul to restore his sight. Paul was known for searching out Christians, arresting them, and even casting his vote to kill them (Acts 26:9-11). If I were Ananias, I would have reminded God about Paul's reputation too. Yes, I am sure that Ananias was uncomfortable, but he was also obedient and did what God told him to do. Ananias placed his hands on Paul; the scales fell from his eyes; he was filled with the Holy Spirit; he was baptized. The rest of the story about Paul's remarkable life is in Acts 22, 26, and the thirteen books of the Bible the Holy Spirit used him to write.

Sometimes God puts us in uncomfortable places because that is where we are needed to make a difference. Ananias, Paul, and Peter were all needed in the place God put them in order to make a difference in their lives and the lives of those they touched. God might keep us in places that are uncomfortable because that is where we are needed. We always need to confirm with God that it is indeed Him leading. If it is Him, He is such a loving God that He will confirm His will to us, and He will go with us. Hallelujah!

Plan of Action:

1. If you have not yet done this, resolve that you are willing to be uncomfortable if He has a work for you that might be out of your normal sphere of comfort. Don't be afraid that He will send you to a third world country. Although we have friends who go there regularly to teach, God doesn't ask that of everyone. (Whew! Thank You, Lord!)

2. If someone presents a new opportunity to you, don't automatically say no. Ask God if the opportunity is from Him. If it is His idea, He will let you know.

3. Praise Him because He loves you and wants to bless you as you bless others. "For my yoke is easy to bear, and the burden I give you is light" (Matthew 11:30 NLT).

Prayer:

Lord, You know that I like my comfortable world, but I don't want to be disobedient if You want me to step out of my comfort zone. I truly want to live in the center of Your will always. Please help me to recognize Your confirmations when You lead me to something or someone new, and please give me the courage to move forward. Since I know how wonderful it is when You use me to bless others, I do want You to use me again, even if it makes me uncomfortable at first. Thank You, my magnificent, great, loving Lord! I pray in the beautiful, powerful name of Jesus. Amen.

CONFIRM YOUR FACTS

Scripture Reading: Luke 7:11-28

"John's disciples told him about all these things [miracles that Christ had performed]. Calling two of them, he sent them to the Lord to ask, 'Are you the one who was to come, or should we expect someone else?'" (Luke 7:18-19).

When we read the quoted Scripture above when John the Baptist sent the men to Jesus to ask if He was the Messiah, let's remember that John the Baptist was Jesus' cousin. He was Elizabeth and Zechariah's son. Don't you think John grew up hearing about the time Mary came to visit his mother and Elizabeth knew that the baby Mary carried was the Messiah? "Elizabeth was filled with the Holy Spirit. In a loud voice she exclaimed, 'Blessed are you among women, and blessed is the child you bear! But why am I so favored, that the mother of my Lord should come to me? As soon as the sound of your greeting reached my ears, the baby in my womb leaped for joy'" (Luke 1:41-44). Most families repeat stories of significant happenings in their lives, and I believe this had to be true of John's family too.

Yet, having heard this over the years, John still wanted and needed to be sure this was not just a proud aunt's and momma's story. If John the Baptist was going to profess this Jesus as the long awaited Messiah, he needed to be sure. He needed to seek out the fact, the confirmation, himself. And so do we.

We are not supposed to take our mother's, our aunt's, or our friend's word that Jesus is the Messiah. We need to confirm that fact for ourselves. How do we do this?

We need only to call Him because He is faithful to answer our call. If we seek Him, He will be found. "Ask and it will be given to you; seek and you will find; knock and the door will be opened" (Matthew 7:7). The Holy Spirit states in several Scriptures what He confirms in Jeremiah 29:13, "You will seek me and find me when you seek me with all your heart." We ask through prayer. We seek Him through prayer and reading the Bible. We talk to other followers of Christ and seek confirmation that He is indeed the Christ. The wonder of wonders is that our God, the God who created the universe, encourages us to seek Him. He wants to have a personal relationship with us. He created us for His glory, and He loves us. What an amazing truth that is!

Also notice Christ's response to John's question. He wasn't offended. In fact, after He tells the disciples what to tell John, He speaks highly of this man, His cousin, who lived in the desert. "I tell you, among those born of women there is no one greater than John; yet the one who is least in the kingdom of God is greater than he" (Luke 7:28).

Our God is not offended when we ask Him questions. He actually wants us to seek Him, to seriously look for Him in our daily lives. We are allowed, even encouraged to confirm that He is our Savior. He created everything, including our brains. He can easily handle our questions as we seek Him with our whole heart.

Plan of Action:

1. If you don't personally know Christ, begin your quest to know Him. He is waiting to answer you.

2. If you do know Him, rejoice that God in His mercy loves you. Do you remember how you came to know Christ as your Savior? Was there someone in particular who was instrumental in introducing you to Him? If you have not done so, you might write them a note of thanks for their faithful service in sharing Christ with you.

Prayer:

Father, we are so very privileged to belong to You. Thank You for loving us and bringing us into Your Kingdom. Please help us to honor You in every part of our lives, and please make us sensitive and obedient when we are to introduce another person to You. We pray in Jesus' name. Amen.

DEPART, DEPART!

Scripture Reading: Psalm 143

"I will instruct you and teach you in the way you should go; I will counsel you and watch over you" (Psalm 32:8).

In our lives, we have to make a myriad of decisions. Some are fairly easy like what to have for dinner. Others are more difficult and of immeasurable importance, such as who to marry, what to do as an occupation, and where to live? For these types of questions, we must wait on the Lord. Since He cares about every aspect of our lives, we can depend on Him to enlighten us. ". . . I am the LORD your God, who teaches you what is best for you, who directs you in the way you should go" (Isaiah 48:17).

Sometimes God decides to move us from one place to another. In this case, we want to be sure that it is His call and not our own discomfort or dissatisfaction with the present conditions. We need to confirm His call to move before we begin to make life altering decisions. Then we can stand on His promises. ". . . I will never leave you nor forsake you" (Joshua 1:5). ". . . The God of heaven will give us success . . . " (Nehemiah 2:20).

I will give you an example from my personal life. Many years ago, my husband, Bill, had a job where a new leader of the corporation was hired. Because Bill was well-liked and had been the prominent representative of the company for two years, the new leader wanted to replace him with someone new who would not have such a strong thumbprint on the company and town. Bill could see that the leader was looking for reasons to replace him, and he took this as a sign that God was directing him to look for a new job, which would mean moving to a new state. Before the new leader arrived, he loved his job. We loved the people in the company and the town. We really didn't want to move unless the Lord was directing us to do so. Consequently, we asked for His confirmation that this was His idea and not ours. The next day in my quiet time, the Scripture Reading was "Depart, depart, go out from there; . . . for the LORD will go before you, and the God of Israel will be your rear guard" (Isaiah 52:11-12 ESV). Wow!

The Lord knew that I would wait on Him for another confirmation that indeed this was His choice for us. After all, this was a very big move (literally) for us. That same morning at the women's Bible study in our church, the Scripture which was chosen by the leader for that day was "Depart, depart, go out from there; . . . for the LORD will go before you, and the God of Israel will be your rear guard" (Isaiah 52:11-12 ESV). Yes, it was the very same Scripture that the Lord had given me that morning during my quiet time with Him alone at home. Mercifully, God gave us further confirmations that my husband was to change jobs, and so Bill gave his notice.

He began interviewing, and the Lord blessed us by putting us right where He wanted us and where we stayed for many years. Yes, it meant moving to another city in another state. But we have learned that there is no place better to be than in the center of God's will. It is recorded in the book of Exodus where Moses said to God "If your Presence does not go with us, do not send us up from here" (Exodus 33:15). This is the way we feel. Wherever we go, we want to be sure that it's where God wants us and that He accompanies us. Of course, because we have accepted Jesus as our Savior and Lord, the Holy Spirit lives in us, and therefore, if we move, God does go with us. We want always, always to be sure that we are where He wants us.

Plan of Action:

1. Don't be afraid to pray specific prayers. God cares about every aspect of your life. He loves for you to come to Him with your needs. Ask Him specifically for whatever you need. If it isn't good for you, His answer will be no. But if you want/need something, ask Him. Specific answers to prayers build your faith. He loves that.

2. One of the ways God answers prayer is in your Bible reading, just like He did for me as I related in this devotional. I was following a daily reading of the Bible, and that particular day was Isaiah 52. Therefore, if you are waiting to hear from God, look for Him to answer in your normal daily Bible reading.

3. Many times He guides through your pastor, Bible study leaders, or friends. Keep your ears open. Often He will give you direction without you even telling others what you are waiting to hear from Him.

Prayer:

Lord, first of all, thank You that You love me and that You care about my life. It still amazes me that You created me. You knit me together in my mother's womb is what is written in Psalm 139. I always want to be where You want me to be. Open my eyes to see Your work and open my ears to hear You clearly. As I walk along in this life You have given me, please help me to honor You in every word and deed. I do love You so very much. In Jesus' name. Amen.

DIVISION IN THE BODY

Scripture Reading: 1 Corinthians 12:12-27

". . . there should be no division in the body, but that its parts should have equal concern for each other. If one part suffers, every part suffers with it; if one part is honored, every part rejoices with it" (1 Corinthians 12:25-26).

"Since we live by the Spirit, let us keep in step with the Spirit. Let us not become conceited, provoking and envying each other" (Galatians 5:25-26).

I have never understood competition between churches. If God is taught/preached as the one true God, if Christ is truly taught/preached as God's only Son and the only way to heaven, if the Holy Spirit is taught/preached as God's Spirit that came to teach and comfort God's people here on earth, if God's Word is taught/preached as God's Word, then why would churches feel it necessary to compete rather than work together? Yet some do. There are enough unbelievers in this world that if we would just obey Christ's great commission, we would have plenty to keep us busy and leave little, if any, time to be distracted by other churches' activities. "Therefore go and make disciples of all nations, baptizing them in the name of the Father and of the Son and of the Holy Spirit, and teaching them to obey everything I have commanded you. And surely I am with you always to the very end of the age" (Matthew 28:19-20). That is a God-given, full-time job for us as individuals and for us as members of a church.

Nevertheless, when there is overt competition among churches, it seems that the people in those churches have forgotten that as Christ's followers, we are members of the same family. We are all on the same team. We just have different jobs to do and different ways of serving. In addition, we may worship in different ways since some people prefer formal services while others prefer the casual. Some churches may have services where every hymn, every Scripture, every word is planned and duly orchestrated, while others may allow for extemporaneous activity. But we are still brothers and sisters-in-Christ, called to go and make disciples.

The Scriptures teach us that although we have a variety of Christian churches in a community, thus giving people a choice where to attend, we need to remember that if one part of the body suffers, all suffer with it. Therefore, those who attend the larger church shouldn't gloat because "their church" is doing well and look down their noses on the other churches because "theirs" is suffering. Instead we should all pray for each other. Every church, just like every person, can use prayer. ". . . Do not think of yourself more highly than you ought . . . " (Romans 12:3). If one church in a community is overflowing with members and resources, the members of that church should not think they have a corner on knowledge or on God's blessings. In the same way, those churches with fewer members should not covet the bounty of the well-attended church. Instead, they should thank God that His Word is being heard by lots of people. They should also pray that indeed His Word is being and continues to be preached and learned in that church. If one church has barely enough members to survive, those churches with more resources should thank God for those few faithful, and again pray that His Word is being preached and learned. If there is a church in the community that is suffering from a scandal, the other churches have the responsibility to pray for the peace, spiritual strength, and well-being of those involved including those who attend the hurting church.

Do we not know that we grieve the Holy Spirit when we speak ill of our brothers and sisters-in-Christ? "Do not let any unwholesome talk come out of your mouths, but only what is helpful for building others up according to their needs, that it may benefit those who listen. And do not grieve the Holy Spirit of God, with whom you were sealed for the day of redemption. Get rid of all bitterness, rage and anger, brawling and slander, along with every form of malice" (Ephesians 4:29-31).

He is grieved when we are haughty. He is grieved when we are divisive. He is grieved when we gossip.

"Finally, all of you, live in harmony with one another; be sympathetic, love as brothers, be compassionate and humble (1 Peter 3:8). Let us follow Paul's instruction as he states in Galatians 6:10: "Therefore, as we have opportunity, let us do good to all people, especially to those who belong to the family of believers."

Our communities can tell when its churches work together in Christian love and harmony. Conversely, they can tell when churches work in competition. "How good and pleasant it is when brothers live together in unity" (Psalm 133:1). Our attitude and behavior should agree with Philippians 2:3: "Do nothing out of selfish ambition or vain conceit, but in humility consider others better than yourselves."

Plan of Action:

1. List 5 churches in your community. If you cannot think of 5, look up churches in the Yellow Pages or on the internet.

2. Take a few moments and lift them by name before the Lord and ask Him to bless them with the power of His Holy Spirit, with the revelation and washing of His Word, and with His strength, wisdom, and the necessary knowledge to do His work. Ask that the Lord bless the pastors and leaders and that He help them to honor Him in every part of their lives.

3. Consider if you have envied another church for any reason. Ask God's forgiveness.

4. Lift before the Lord the name of the church where you attend. Pray the same prayer for it that you prayed for the other 5.

Prayer:

Father, please forgive me for looking at other churches with envy and judgment. Please remind me to pray for them when I hear of hurting hearts, a scandal, a need, and even a reason to rejoice. Please help the churches throughout the world to begin to love each other and work together in unity to Your glory. I pray 1 Thessalonians 3:12 for Your church, Lord. "May the Lord make our love increase and overflow for each other and for everyone else, just as ours does for you." In Jesus' name. Amen.

ENTERTAINING STRANGERS

Scripture Reading: Acts 2:42-47

"Keep on loving each other as brothers. Do not forget to entertain strangers for by so doing some people have entertained angels without knowing it" (Hebrews 13:1-2).

As I have mentioned in some of my other writings, because of my husband's job and personality, we frequently entertain people in our home. Often, the first time that I meet our guests is at our front door when they arrive at our home.

I sincerely wish that I could say that I always prepare for these gatherings with joy in my heart and eagerness to meet new people. But that would not be true. I perform the tasks involved with practicing hospitality with care, attention to detail, and prayer, but not always with joy.

Just recently, when my husband and I were attending a national convention, we ran into one of these former guests/strangers and were greeted as though we were exceptionally close friends. The warmth exuded was genuine and lovely. We could tell this gentleman was sincerely pleased to see us and even took us into a confidence which resulted in a request for prayer.

I am grateful for this experience because the next time I am preparing a gathering for strangers, I'll remember this gentleman, and I'll do the work with the understanding that we will very likely be entertaining future friends. I love when the Lord adjusts my attitude. What a treat!

God is so good!

Plan of Action:

1. Do you have a duty that you fulfill with dread?

2. Ask the Lord to adjust your attitude and give you a vision for the possible results of your work.

3. Resolve to serve Him with His grace completing whatever task He sets before you according to the Colossians 3:12: "Therefore as God's chosen people, holy and dearly loved, clothe yourselves with compassion, kindness, humility, gentleness and patience."

Prayer:

Lord, thank You so much for the gracious way You help us to adjust our thoughts! I thank You for enlarging our vision to see what You have in store for our lives. Please forgive us for our selfish thoughts and behavior. You served as a servant. Please help us to do the same with grace. Thank You for always helping us. I pray in Jesus' name. Amen.

FEAR NOT

Scripture Reading: Genesis 3

"And the LORD God commanded the man, 'You are free to eat from any tree in the garden; but you must not eat from the tree of the knowledge of good and evil, for when you eat of it you will surely die'" (Genesis 2:16-17).

Don't you wish we were ignorant about evil? Have you ever seen something evil on TV and wished you could "unsee" it? I saw a television show where it told of the evil done by one person to another, and though I didn't actually see the evil being acted out, I imagined it, and now I wish I could "unsee" it.

If Adam and Eve hadn't disobeyed God by eating from the tree of the knowledge of good and evil, we wouldn't have to know about evil. In fact, there would be no evil. When we get to heaven, there will be no evil. Meanwhile, we can rest on 1 Peter 5:7 "Cast all your anxiety on him because he cares for you." And how does He care for us? "It is the LORD who goes before you. He will be with you; he will not leave you or forsake you. Do not fear or be dismayed" (Deuteronomy 31:8 ESV). Add to that Scripture Psalm 139:5 "You go before me and follow me. You place your hand of blessing on my head" (NLT). No matter where we go, God is there with us and His hand of blessing is on our heads.

To a certain extent, we can protect ourselves from knowing evil. "I will set before my eyes no vile thing" (Psalm 101:3a). We can pick and choose what we watch on the television, at the movie theatre, etc. We can also pick and choose what books we read. God wants us to make good choices. But where evil is concerned, He wants us to remain as children. In other words, innocent and unknowing. "In regard to evil be infants, but in your thinking be adults" (1 Corinthians 14:20b). Sometimes we may happen upon evil while watching a show or reading a book that we thought would be safe. Isn't that a disappointment? Remember what God tells us through the Apostle Paul in Philippians 4:8: "And now, dear brothers and sisters, one final thing. Fix your thoughts on what is true, and honorable, and right, and pure, and lovely, and admirable. Think about things that are excellent and worthy of praise" (NLT).

When the random shootings started happening in malls and even churches, I found verses 7 and 8 of Psalm 138 helpful and encouraging: "Though I walk in the midst of trouble, you preserve my life; you stretched out your hand against the anger of my foes, with your right hand you save me. The LORD will fulfill his purpose for me; your love, O LORD, endures forever—do not abandon the works of your hand." I decided that was a good Scripture to memorize. Just knowing and speaking God's Word is calming, and I appreciate God's promises that He will fight our enemies. We can rest in Him to protect us and to always be with us until it is our turn to be ushered to heaven. It is reassuring to know that God is never caught by surprise (Job 14:5).

Although the first man and woman disobeyed God and let sin enter the world, God wants only His best for us. His good wins over evil. "Fear not, for I am with you: be not dismayed, for I am your God; I will strengthen you, I will help you, I will uphold you with my righteous right hand" (Isaiah 41:10 ESV). We belong to God. In fact, we are His children whom He loves so much that He allowed His precious Son to die so that our heavenly Father could have many sons and daughters (John 3:16; 2 Cor. 6:18).

Plan of Action:

1. Choose carefully what you watch on TV and what you read. Avoid evil as much as you can.

2. You might want to invest your time in some research on that book, television show, or movie before you expose yourself to it. There are lots of really good Christian books from which you can choose if you want to stay on the safe side. Otherwise, make good decisions as the Christian you are.

Prayer:

Lord, I would love for You to erase the vile things that I have seen and imagined. There is so much beauty in this world where You have placed me. Help me to camp on those things. I ask that You help me to remain as a child—innocent where evil is concerned. Give me wisdom as I make choices as to what I watch and read. Thank You, Lord. I pray in Jesus' name. Amen.

GPS (GLOBAL POSITIONING SYSTEM)

Scripture Reading: Exodus 13:1-18

"When Pharaoh let the people go, God did not lead them on the road through the Philistine country, though that was shorter. For God said, 'If they face war, they might change their minds and return to Egypt'" (Exodus 13:17).

My husband and I were using a GPS when traveling south from our home in Kentucky. We were on a major highway when the GPS told us to take the next exit. Because we trusted our knowledge of the area more than we trusted the GPS, we chose to ignore its instruction and continued on the highway. We soon realized why the GPS told us to exit several miles back. The traffic ahead of us was at a standstill.

On the other hand, we all have stories of how the GPS misguided us. One of my favorites is when I was traveling from western Kentucky to eastern Kentucky. I stopped off to get a cup of coffee. When back in my car, I pressed "Start" on the GPS, and it proceeded to take me to a horse farm just outside of Lexington. The system announced that I had reached my destination! Nope. Not even close!

Exodus 13 was my Scripture Reading earlier today, and when I came to Exodus 13:17-18, the Lord reminded me of the travel episodes I mentioned above. Before Global Positioning Systems, there was God's pillar of cloud and His pillar of fire. Unlike our Global Positioning Systems, both were one hundred percent reliable. I don't know if the Israelites knew God was taking them the long way to the Promised Land, but if they did, I am sure they would have questioned His navigational instructions. After all, we know that God had them wandering around for forty years because of their rebellion and grumbling against Him (Numbers 13:26-14:35).

Plan of Action:

1. Ask yourself if you are guilty of second guessing God's guidance for your life. If you are, look up Psalm 32:8. If God tells you that He will teach you the way you should go, you can believe Him. He is all powerful, supremely dependable, and cannot lie. If you need to see more Scriptures promising His guidance, read Isaiah 48:17 and Psalm 23.

2. Ask yourself if you trust God. If not, look up Proverbs 3:5-6. We may not be able to fully trust any human being, but we most certainly can trust God. After all, He made us, He loves us, and He wants to take care of us. Read Psalm 139:1-18, 23-24.

3. Ask yourself why God sent Jesus to take on your sins. Look at John 3:16. Who does God love? He loves the world so much that He sent Jesus to take on the world's sins, and that includes you and your sins. Who does God save from hell? Whoever believes in Jesus. Do you believe in Jesus? If so, you will have eternal life with God the Father, Jesus the Son, and the Holy Spirit.

Prayer:

Lord, I submit to You. Please teach me, lead me, and save me from the sinful ways of the world. Help me to trust You, and please help me to discern Your voice from all others. Thank You for creating me and loving me. Please open my eyes to see Your way clearly and open my ears to hear You clearly. Help me to willfully follow You. In Jesus' name I pray. Amen.

GLORIFY GOD

Scripture Reading: Psalm 16:5-11

"So whether you eat or drink or whatever you do, do it all for the glory of God" (1 Corinthians 10:31).

Have you ever heard of Llon Specht? Or Foote, Cone and Belding? Or Kennedy+Weiden? I would be surprised if you were familiar with those names unless you were in the advertising business. While Llon Specht is a person who worked at Manhattan Ad Agency, the others are actually advertising agencies, and they don't exist to make a name for themselves. They exist to make a name for the companies or people they represent.

Do you recognize the phrase "Because You're Worth It"? Llon Specht coined the phrase in 1971 when working for Manhattan Ad Agency. What about the motto "When you care enough to send the very best"? Foote and Belding created this in 1934 for Hallmark. How about "Just Do It!"? Kennedy+Weiden Ad Agency created that for Nike. Probably none of us recognize the names of the advertising agencies, but most of us recognize the taglines and could connect them with the product. My point is that these agencies fulfilled their purpose by making their product famous rather than promoting themselves.

In the same way, we are not supposed to be promoting ourselves. Instead we should be promoting our Lord. We should represent Him so that by our actions, we focus all attention and glory on Him. I am not suggesting that every other word in a conversation is Jesus or prayer or amen. I am suggesting that we are sensitive to people around us and their needs and worries. We may have an opportunity to say, "I am sorry about your mother's illness. I will pray for her." After we have been with people for a short while, they should know we are Christians. Really it only requires a gentle word here, a kind word there. We are to let the world know that we know the Great Physician, the Miracle Worker, the Peace Giver, who is also a Loving Father.

According to the Westminster Catechism, we have the privilege of glorifying God and enjoying Him forever. We can do that in our everyday life as we exhibit the fruit of the Holy Spirit in our behavior: love, joy, peace, patience, kindness, goodness, faithfulness, gentleness, and self-control (Galatians 5:22-23).

Plan of Action:

1. What a wonderful task we have in glorifying God and enjoying Him. Sit back and let your mind focus on our gracious, loving, powerful God. Glorify Him and enjoy Him. You might want to look again at Psalm 16:5-11.

2. Isaiah 43:4 "You are precious and honored in my sight, and . . . I love you." Here the Lord is speaking to Israel, but it is also true for His children today. Remember that God loved us so much that He allowed Christ to die for your sins and my sins. You are precious to Him. I am precious to Him. That leaves me almost speechless. Let's praise Him and thank Him.

3. You may think that allowing the Holy Spirit to shine through will go unnoticed. Take another look at the world right now. People are explosively angry today. Kindness stands out. Patience is not in abundance. Aren't you drawn to someone who is gentle? Generally speaking don't we tend to love people we know love us? I know I tend to love people who love my husband and my children. Let God do His work through you. You will be blessed and amazed.

Prayer:

Lord, I am so touched by Your kindness and generosity. To think that I am precious to You, oh my beloved God, I am so very grateful for You and Your love. Open my eyes to see all possibilities to introduce others to You. I ask that I represent You so well that others will want what I have, and You will help me to draw them to You. I thank You that You can do even more than I can think or imagine. In Jesus' beautiful, powerful name. Amen.

GOD'S GUIDANCE

Scripture Reading: Psalm 121

"I will instruct you and teach you in the way you should go; I will counsel you and watch over you" (Psalm 32:8).

"Ask and it will be given to you; seek and you will find; knock and the door will be opened to you. For everyone who asks receives; he who seeks finds; and to him who knocks, the door will be opened" (Matthew 7:7-8).

When asking God if He wanted me to write a third *Lord, It's Time for Just You and Me*, He gave me three confirmations that His answer was yes. One came as He reminded me that I had several unfinished pieces that He had started with me when I was writing Book 2. I had forgotten that He leads us step by step, and I hadn't taken the next step by working on what He'd already given me. So why would He give me new material? He expected me to be a good steward and reap from what He had already sown in me. I reread them and decided that they were indeed material that He had given me. They were worth completing.

Second, still looking to Him for further confirmation that I should write a third book, I finished my work on the book for the day and started my study of Spanish with my language app. One of the first questions for me to translate from English to Spanish was, "Do you already know the subject of your next book?" Some might say, "Oh that was just coincidence." I don't think so. I was waiting on His direction about starting a third book. I had prayed. I had begun revision on the work He had given me years ago. I continued my questioning, seeking His desire. And He answered through my next, unrelated work, my study of Spanish.

Third, during the time when I was starting to work on the third devotional, I was at home after just attending our worship service. The Scripture that had been preached was Matthew 7:7-8, which I have quoted above. As I started work on my devotional, the Scriptural reference of the piece I had begun to revise was Matthew 7:7-8. That was not a coincidence. That was the communication of the Holy Spirit confirming to me that He did indeed want me to write the third *Lord, It's Time for Just You and Me*.

I tell you this because I want you to be comfortable asking for God's guidance and then watching for His answers. I am a child of His just like you are. If I can ask Him for guidance, so can you. If He is so generous to answer my questions, He will do the same for you.

There are many Scriptures in addition to the two I quoted at the beginning of this piece that tell us He wants us to ask for His help. Here are just four more. "I know, O LORD, that a man's life is not his own; it is not for man to direct his steps" (Jeremiah 10:23). "If any of you lacks wisdom, he should ask God, who gives generously to all without finding fault, and it will be given to him" (James 1:5). "Show me your ways, O LORD, teach me your paths; guide me in your truth and teach me, for you are God my Savior, and my hope is in you all day long (Psalm 25:4-5). "Call to me and I will answer you. I'll tell you marvelous and wondrous things that you could never figure out on your own" (Jeremiah 33:3 *The Message*). Isn't that a remarkable Scripture? I want God to tell me marvelous and wondrous things I could never figure out on my own.

Ask for His guidance. He will not fail you.

Plan of Action:

1. I suggest that you write down something you have been wondering if you are supposed to become involved in. Ask God to guide you. Then wait to see His directions.

2. With each confirmation He gives you, write it down. This way you will have it to look at in case you question your decision later.

Prayer:

Father, to think that You, the God of the universe, the God Who created everyone and everything cares enough for me that You want to help me make decisions, that You want to direct my steps, that You want me to communicate with You. I am in awe of this relationship that You have with Your created ones. Please help me to honor You in all that I do, and please do remind me to ask for Your guidance in all of my life for the rest of my life. Thank You, Lord. In Jesus' name. Amen.

GOD'S WORK IN US

Scripture Reading: Romans 8:28-30

"And we, who with unveiled faces all reflect the Lord's glory, are being transformed into his likeness with ever-increasing glory, which comes from the Lord, who is Spirit" (2 Corinthians 3:18).

"For we are God's workmanship, created in Christ Jesus to do good works, which God prepared in advance for us to do" (Ephesians 2:10).

It is a well-known fact that we can control and even alter some of our outward appearance. Since most of us want to present ourselves in the best possible way, we keep our bodies clean and our hair detangled. We maintain modesty in dress and behavior. We exercise our bodies to keep fit, and we even work to change bad eating habits. For those who want to reduce the effects of the aging process and are willing to invest the money and endure the pain, cosmetic procedures are an option. For those of us who don't want to deal with the pain or expense of those procedures, we let gravity and age have their way and avoid mirrors. In an effort to improve the way we are received by others, we may even go to such lengths as to practice changing our speech patterns to get rid of unacceptable use of slang or easily misconstrued regional phrases.

Certainly our physical appearance is affected by our faith and trust in God. Our body language and our faces mirror the stress or peace we have within us. We attend church worship and Bible study to help maintain our relationship with our Lord.

All of the things listed above are a result of effort on our part to change our appearance. Yet as much as we work on improving ourselves, the most important part of who we are is purely a result of the work of the Holy Spirit, not a result of our own effort. As we spend time in His Word and let Him do His work with us, submitting to His will, we change. He changes us. He can revive us and make us wise. "The law of the LORD is perfect, reviving the soul. The statutes of the LORD are trustworthy, making wise the simple" (Psalm 19:7). "Your commands are always with me and make me wiser than my enemies" (Psalm 119:98). He can take uneducated men and women and make them courageous and knowledgeable. "When they saw the courage of Peter and John and realized that they were unschooled, ordinary men, they were astonished and they took note that these men had been with Jesus" (Acts 4:13). Peter and John spent time with Jesus. Spending time with our Lord changes us too.

The amazing and wonderful fact is that He does the work in us. He works with our inner man and woman to help us to reflect Him. "Don't copy the behavior and customs of this world, but let God transform you into a new person by changing the way you think. Then you will know what God wants you to do, and you will know how good and pleasing and perfect his will really is" (Romans 12:2 NLT). The Scripture says, "Let God transform you . . ." He does the work. We read His Word and He changes us. We spend time in prayer and worship, and He changes us.

We read in Romans 8:28 and 30 that He called us. In John 15:16 Christ discloses, "You did not choose me, but I chose you and appointed you to go and bear fruit—fruit that will last . . ." In Romans 8:29, the apostle Paul tells us that God "foreknew" us. He saved us by His gift of rebirth because of His mercy and grace, not because we earned salvation by doing the right things or by exhibiting the correct behavior (Titus 3:5). "For it is by grace you have been saved, through faith—and this not from yourselves, it is the gift of God—not by works, so that no one can boast" (Ephesians 2:8-9). He predestined us to be conformed to the likeness of His Son (Romans 8:29). It is in His plan for our lives to be conformed to the likeness of Christ. That could not happen on our own effort or merit. Romans 8:30 confirms that He justified us. When we accepted Christ's shed blood as the sacrifice for our sins, He declared us innocent, worthy of His forgiveness and love, and qualified to receive the inheritance of His saints (Colossians 1:12). He glorified us (Romans 8:30), and that glory "comes from the Lord, who is the Spirit" (2 Corinthians 3:18). We are glorified and exhibit the fruit of the Holy Spirit because we are in Christ, and Christ is in us (John 15:5). Ultimately, He will literally transform our human bodies "so that they will be like his glorious body" (Philippians 3:21). In our human form, our lives begin as embryos whose very existence depends on our mothers. When we are born, we need help in nearly everything we do. As we grow, we gradually become more independent and self-sufficient. Then, as we become older adults, most of our bodies become encumbered with physical ailments and limitations. Ho hum! But God's Word tells us that when we arrive in heaven, He will transform our bodies to be like His glorious body. What an encouragement!

"Charm is deceptive, and beauty is fleeting; but a woman who fears the LORD is to be praised" (Proverbs 31:30). What we have in this human, physical body is fleeting. But what He gives us is eternal life. It is His gift to us, and He will continue to work in us, transforming us to His likeness, until we see Christ face to face (Philippians 1:6).

Plan of Action:

1. Let's thank God that He is supernaturally changing us to be more and more like Christ.
2. Praise God for His wonderful plans for your life.

Prayer:

Lord, Your ways are far above ours. We are amazed and grateful that You desire to work with us, and You declare us worthy of Your love. Please help us to honor You with this life You have given us. In Jesus' name. Amen.

THE GOOD SAMARITAN

Scripture Reading: Luke 10:25-37

"But a Samaritan, as he journeyed, came to where he was, and when he saw him, he had compassion" (Luke 10:33 ESV).

Most people are familiar with this story. I have heard it preached and have read it numerous times. However, this time when I read it, I noticed that as the priest and Levite passed the beaten man, the Bible doesn't attribute compassion to either of them. Granted, they may have thought he was already dead and didn't want to defile themselves by touching a corpse. But even if they thought the man was dead, shouldn't they have felt compassion for the beaten man? If they had, I believe the Bible would have noted that. The Samaritan did have compassion for him and helped him most generously.

You may remember that Samaritans were scorned by the Jews because their kind of worship and place of worship were different than that of Orthodox Judaism. Since it was a Samaritan who helped the man, that made the story even more poignant to the listening Jews.

Jesus asked who of these proved to be a neighbor (love your neighbor as yourself)? The lawyer answered, "The one who showed him mercy" (Luke 10:37 ESV). Jesus said, "Go, and do likewise" (Luke 10:37). Jesus was showing that to this Samaritan, any person who needed help was his neighbor, and that should be true for the lawyer, and it should be true for us. Our prayer should be that when we see someone who is hurting, we will have compassion on him and help him.

Plan of Action:

1. As Christians we are to have compassion for those in need. It may not be a life-or-death situation as it was in The Good Samaritan story. It may be someone who has an ill spouse and could use a meal he didn't have to prepare. Once, after I had had surgery, one of my friends brought us a roasted chicken, a bag of salad, and bakery cookies from the grocery store and said, "We're going to pretend that I made this." Then we laughed. But we appreciated it even if it wasn't homemade.

2. Remember that ministry is not always convenient. You may be in the middle of an activity when someone who is just learning about the Bible calls with a question. Be ready to take the time to answer her.

Prayer:

Lord, please help me to serve You wherever You place me, and please help me to have compassion for those in need. Remind me that sometimes I can put my schedule aside to help someone, even if it is just answering a question about faith or the Bible. Shape me to be available to anyone that You bring to me. Please never let me miss an opportunity to serve You as You want me to. Thank You, Lord, for continuing to teach me. I pray in Jesus' name. Amen.

THE GOOD SHEPHERD

Scripture Reading: John 10:1-30

"I am the good shepherd. The good shepherd lays down his life for his sheep" (John 10:11).

In my written work called "God's Favor," in my first devotional *Lord, It's Time for Just You and Me*, I wrote about the time when the angel announced the good news to the shepherds in the fields that Christ the Lord had been born in a stable in Bethlehem (Luke 2:8-20). I was reading that Scripture again today and had a new revelation. At least it was new to me. I just realized that God chose to announce the birth of His Son, the Good Shepherd, to the *shepherds* in the fields. When the shepherds looked at Jesus in the manger, they were looking into the eyes of the Good Shepherd. Don't you know they sensed they were in God's presence?

Their visit to Bethlehem was a result of an angelic announcement of Christ's birth. From the time they started their journey until they saw Jesus face to face, they must have been filled with anticipation of what they would find. An angel had told them of Christ's birth, and then "Suddenly a great company of heavenly host appeared with the angel, praising God and saying, 'Glory to God in the highest heaven, and on earth peace to men on whom his favor rests'" (Luke 2:13-14). They went from doing their job as shepherds in the field to visiting the Lord God Almighty. Imagine what they must have felt. I believe it was beyond description.

We too get to know the Good Shepherd. He loves us and cares for us, His flock. "Come, let us bow down in worship, let us kneel before the LORD our Maker; for he is our God and we are the people of his pasture, the flock under his care" (Psalm 95:6-7). He is the Gate (John 10:7) through whom we may go to the Father (John 14:6) and receive salvation (John 10:9). Our Good Shepherd gave His life for us (John 10:11), and because of that, no one can snatch us out of His hand (John 10:28). We are His sheep, members of His family (Psalm 100:3 and Ephesians 1:4-6) today and eternally.

Plan of Action:

1. Take a few minutes to think of all the ways a shepherd looks after his flock. Now consider that the Creator of the universe, your Good Shepherd, is looking after you in the same ways. Trust Him. You couldn't be in better hands.

2. Spend just a few more minutes thanking Him for watching after you, providing for you, loving you enough to have given His life for you.

Prayer:

O, my precious Lord, how can I ever thank You enough for all You have done for me? How can I possibly thank You for all You continually do for me? I look back on my life and remember accidents that almost happened but You prevented them. I am sure, Lord, that You have snatched my life out of peril so many times. And, Lord, I think of all You have taught me from Your Word. How can I possibly thank You? You know how very grateful I am. With all I am, Lord, I thank You. In Jesus' name. Amen.

GRACE EXTENDERS

Scripture Reading: Psalm 100

"For it is by grace you have been saved, through faith—and this not from yourselves, it is the gift of God—not by works, so that no one can boast" (Ephesians 2:8-9).

Have you ever met a grace extender? Maybe one of your friends is a grace extender, or perhaps you are one. I have a new friend whom I characterize as a grace extender. She effervesces with praise to God for the works of other believers. While other people, both believers and unbelievers, may express disapproval of another person's ministry, she leads with, "Praise God for his gift. Isn't it wonderful what he is doing? It would be difficult for me. But praise God for calling him to this work." She lives Psalm 100, and she helps me appreciate God's call and purpose in His children's lives. She is a joy to be around! I praise God for her. We should all be grace extenders.

Of course, God is the ultimate and perfect grace extender. Just as in Ephesians 2:8-9, quoted above, God gave us His grace and His faith to save us eternally. We will be able to live with Him in heaven forever because of the gifts of His grace and faith. "Now it is God who makes both us and you stand firm in Christ. He anointed us, set his seal of ownership on us, and put his Spirit in our hearts as a deposit, guaranteeing what is to come" (2 Corinthians 1:21-22). Later in Paul's letter to the Corinthians he said, "And God is able to make all grace abound in you, so that in all things at all times, having all that you need, you will abound in every good work" (2 Corinthians 9:8). Since He gives us these gifts freely, we too should freely offer His grace to others, and we should pray for our unbelieving friends that He give them the faith they need to accept Christ as their Savior and Lord. Jesus said in John 6:44, "No one can come to me unless the Father who sent me draws him." I pray that God will draw my unbelieving friends to Him.

Plan of Action:

1. Think of your friends who are unbelievers. List them in your phone or on paper, and ask God to draw them to Him. Write the date of your prayer next to their names, and wait to see the Lord work.

2. Decide today that you will be a grace extender. When people are around a grace extender, they will be less self-conscious because they know she will overlook their flaws. In fact, they know you are not looking for flaws. After all, we are all humans who are working with God on a journey to be more like Christ (Ephesians 4:13). All of us have rough areas that need to be smoothed by the work of the Holy Spirit, in and by His grace. Rather than finding faults in others, I am truly doing well to address my own flaws. I pray as David did in Psalm 139:23-24. "Search me, O God, and know my heart; test me and know my anxious thoughts. Point out anything in me that offends you, and lead me along the path of everlasting life" (NLT).

Prayer:

Lord, I ask that You help me to extend freely Your grace to others. I know that I am nowhere near perfect, and I will improve only by Your grace. Please point out times when I tend to judge unfairly. I know there are times I am to judge, as when someone misquotes Your Word. Then with Your love and tender speech, You will allow me to correct the misinformation. I also know that there are many times that I jump to judge when it isn't You leading me, but me running ahead of You. I want You to give me Your view of matters and people. You know when we need correction and when we need to have grace extended. I don't want to be unnecessarily negative. Thank You, Lord, for Your grace, Your grace extenders, Your love, Your forgiveness, Your willingness to correct us. I love You, Lord. Please help me to be a grace extender too. I pray in Jesus' name. Amen.

GROUP DYNAMICS

Scripture Reading: 2 Corinthians 5:17-21

"For we are the aroma of Christ to God among those who are being saved and among those who are perishing, to one a fragrance from death to death, to the other a fragrance from life to life" (2 Corinthians 2:15-16 ESV).

Have you noticed that the normal behavior of crass people changes because of your presence in a group? You have seen the direction in which they would normally take a discussion, but as they glance at you, the off color remarks are held back. This is not a coincidence, and it is not thinking more of yourself than you ought. It is because you have the Holy Spirit living in you, and even if others don't know why they are restrained, you and God know why. When God is present, sin is recognized for the evil it is. I love the way 2 Corinthians 3:18 is in *The Living Bible*, "But we Christians have no veil over our faces; we can be mirrors that brightly reflect the glory of the Lord."

This is not a time to feel smug or self-righteous. This is a time to praise God for His work and to ask that He work in these people's lives. No one is out of God's reach to save. "He [the Lord] is patient with you, not wanting anyone to perish, but everyone to come to repentance" (2 Peter 3:9b).

Many years ago, my husband had an acquaintance with whom he would occasionally have breakfast before starting work. They had similar jobs, and that gave them a commonality. One evening, he and his wife and my husband

and I went out to dinner together. Almost every other word out of this man's mouth was foul. By the time we arrived home, I felt like I needed to take a shower. From then on if he was in a group, I avoided him. I wish I could tell you that I prayed for him. But I didn't. I just judged him as a lost soul.

Several months later, when I accompanied my husband to breakfast at his usual place, this man was already there. As he made his way over to me, I groaned inside. He sat beside me and shared that he had accepted Christ as his Savior in a church the night before. I could tell that he was serious and joyful. I was shocked and ashamed that I hadn't thought to pray for him. I don't believe I ever said anything about being a believer, but you see, he knew. We have remained friends over the years, and I am still in awe at how God changed him overnight. No more foul language or "good ol' boy" nudges. He became active in his church and is still today. He is a fine, dignified gentleman. No one would ever guess that he was the man I met those many years ago.

I tell you this story because I truly believe that no one is out of God's reach. Look at Saul whom we know best as Paul. He was actively working against believers when he was blinded on the road to Damascus by Jesus. Jesus chose him to be an apostle. He served God diligently until his death. Again, no one is out of God's reach. I sing His praises!

Plan of Action:

1. Do you have someone in your life that you do not like, and you are pretty sure he/she is not a Christian? Right now, pray for his/her salvation. Ask the Lord to make this person a new creation. 2 Corinthians 5:17 says "If anyone is in Christ, he is a new creation; the old has gone, the new has come!"

2. Remember that in every group, you represent Christ. Sometimes you will say something that makes it plain that you are a Christian, and other times you won't say anything. But whether you refer to your Savior or not, you are His representative. Let your behavior and your words glorify and honor Him. I used to tell our kids when they went out of the house to play or to school, "Remember that you represent our family, and you represent our Lord." When we realize that, it gives us a new perspective of how to live our lives.

3. As you go through your day, keep this Scripture in mind: "Always give yourselves fully to the work of the Lord, because you know that your labor in the Lord is not in vain" (1 Corinthians 15:58).

Prayer:

Lord, I am absolutely amazed at Your work! Please help me to always represent You well. Remind me to pray for people that You place in my life who don't seem to know You. When I am about to groan silently about their behavior, nudge me to pray for them instead. I love You, Lord. Thank You for loving me. In Jesus' name. Amen.

HAVE YOU TOLD ANYONE LATELY?

Scripture Reading: Luke 8:26-39

Jesus said to him, "'Return to your home and tell how much God has done for you.' So the man went away and told all over town how much Jesus had done for him" (Luke 8:38-39).

The account in the **Scripture Reading** for today is one of my favorite stories in the New Testament. You may think it odd that this is one of my favorite stories. But when I see this man who was so demon possessed that he had been " . . . kept under guard and bound with chains and shackles, but he would break the bonds and be driven by the demon into the desert" (Luke 8:29 ESV), my heart breaks for him. His condition looked hopeless. This had been going on for a long time, and the end of such torture seemed impossible.

And then came Jesus. Yes, and then came Jesus. He cast out the legion of demons, sent them to the herd of pigs, and the man who hadn't known peace for a very long time was healed. I love the picture the Scripture shows when the people from the surrounding city and country came to see what had happened. They " . . . found the man from whom the demons had gone out, sitting at Jesus' feet, dressed and in his right mind . . . " (Luke 8:35).

I also love the report that when Jesus got into the boat to leave, this same man begged Jesus to let him go with Him. But Jesus replied, "Return home and tell how much God has done for you" (Luke 8:39). And he did just that.

Thank You, Lord!

Isn't that an absolutely amazing story?! In it we see the absolute, supreme power of Jesus, as well as His loving compassion for mankind. Just as it breaks our hearts to see tortured people in this world, it breaks Christ's heart. He wants all mankind to live free of demons—all demons. Remember "Jesus Christ is the same yesterday and today and forever" (Hebrews 13:8). He heals even today. What a wonderful Savior we have!

Have you told anyone lately how much God has done for you?

Plan of Action:

1. Ask the Lord to prepare you and give you the courage to tell others how much God has done for you. Then look for opportunities to do so.

2. Remember that there are people who are as tormented as the man in today's Scripture. They may not be in visible chains, but they are in chains all the same, and they would love to be set free. Introduce them to the Person who can heal them.

Prayer:

Lord, thank You for this wonderful account of this man who was so horribly tortured until You set him free. Open our eyes to see others who are also tortured, and give us the words and the courage to introduce them to You, our Savior. Thank You that You care for all You have created. Help us to care for them too and to give them the Way to freedom. In Jesus' name. Amen.

HIS LOVE ENDURES FOREVER

Scripture Reading: Psalm 136

"'Though the mountains be shaken and the hills be removed,
yet my unfailing love for you will not be shaken
nor my covenant of peace be removed,'
says the LORD" (Isaiah 54:10).

Psalm 136 in the **Scripture Reading** above begins "Give thanks to the LORD, for he is good. *His love endures forever.*" Then verses 4-9 tell us that He created the world and "*His love endures forever.*" As the Israelites went to war against many kings, God handed the kings and their countries over as an inheritance to His beloved people because *His love endures forever.* We too can revel in that love because we have been grafted into His family through Christ (Romans 11:11-24). God adopted us because of Jesus (Ephesians 1:5).

The psalmist by the Holy Spirit's inspiration recalls what the Lord of lords did for His people, and we can see a small picture of His magnificence. This Psalm reminds us of what our God has done for us and what He does for us today. "Nothing is impossible with God" (Luke 1:37).

Zephaniah 3:17 "The LORD your God is with you, he is mighty to save. He will take great delight in you, he will quiet you with his love, he will rejoice over you with singing." Can you picture our Lord delighting in us, rejoicing and singing over us? Why? Because His love endures forever. How much does God love us? "God so loved the world [that includes you and me] that he gave his one and only Son, that whoever believes in him [that is us] shall not perish but have eternal life" (John 3:16).

Plan of Action:

1. Let your mind dwell on the fact that God rejoices and sings over you.

2. I am sure that you have heard of the Great Commission which Jesus gave to His disciples and that includes us. "Go and make disciples of all nations, baptizing them in the name of the Father and of the Son and of the Holy Spirit, and teaching them to obey everything I have commanded you. And surely I am with you always, to the very end of the age" (Matthew 28:19-20). Are you willing to make disciples? Have you ever shared your faith in Christ with anyone? Let's agree with the apostle Paul who asked "That God may open a door for our message, so that we may . . . proclaim it clearly . . . " (Colossians 4:3-4). Ask God who in your circle of friends doesn't seem to know Christ. Picture yourself introducing them to Jesus as you share your story with them. Remember the story needs to be more about Christ's work in you and less about you alone.

Prayer:

My Lord and my God, I am overwhelmed when I realize that You delight in me and that You rejoice over me with singing. What a mighty voice You must have! I look forward to hearing it when I am in heaven with You. Father, if there is someone in my circle of friends or acquaintances that You are preparing to receive the Good News that Jesus died for their sins, move me, Lord, to speak Your words at the right time. Guard my mouth so I don't jump ahead of You. But also spur me on at the right time. I do so love You, Lord. Help me always to bless You. In Jesus' name. Amen.

HIS SOVEREIGNTY

Scripture Reading: Psalm 71

"Since my youth, God, you have taught me, and to this day I declare your marvelous deeds" (Psalm 71:17).

Today, the Lord showed me again how He has guided my husband and me over the years. We were remembering specifically His nudging us to move from Kansas City, where we had lived all of our lives, to Pikeville, Kentucky, which we knew nothing about. Bill was offered the job of Chair of the Department of Medicine to help get a fledgling medical school established. We had no desire to move. Bill had a very busy medical practice in the Kansas City area. We were involved in a wonderful church. We were close to family. We had lots of friends. We were settled. Nevertheless, we knew that we had to hear from God about this possible, albeit drastic, change in our lives.

Day after day, I prayed and searched the Scriptures, and day after day, the Lord gave me Scriptures which spoke of Mount Zion. To this point, we hadn't noticed any consecutive references to mountains in the Scriptures before the Pikeville offer. After several days, we were sure that His continual reference to Mt. Zion was one of many confirmations that He wanted us to move to the Appalachian Mountains of Kentucky, our new mission field. This happened in 1998.

Skip forward to the present. Over breakfast, Bill and I considered the many times since then that God guided us to move, and the wonderful experiences He allowed us to have, along with the precious people who became our friends. We were awed at how He, our Sovereign, had directed us throughout our lives. We know we have free will to choose our own way, but His Word promises that if we ask Him, He will direct our steps (Psalm 32:8; Isaiah 48:17). He has certainly done that for us.

After our discussion at breakfast, I headed for my office for my quiet time with the Lord. My Scripture for the day was Psalm 68: 15-16: "The mountains of Bashan are majestic mountains . . . Why gaze in envy, O rugged mountains, at the mountain where God chooses to reign, where the LORD himself will dwell forever?" God didn't call us to serve Him in the Rockies. Instead, God called us to the smaller mountains in Pikeville, Kentucky. In the Scripture above, we see that God chose the smaller mountain where He would dwell forever. We believe that God wanted to encourage us again that indeed our presence in the Appalachian Mountains was where He wanted us for many years.

We know that God doesn't always use the brightest or the flashiest humans to do His remarkable work. That is obvious in His choosing us, two of His flawed and unremarkable servants, to move to Kentucky to help develop a medical school and to serve as His ambassadors in a new location. Gracious God that He is, He had already established a wonderful church in Pikeville, full of humble servants who prayed for us, worked with us, and loved us. We praise Him for sovereignly working through His church, whether it is in Kansas City or Pikeville!

Plan of Action:

1. Are you in the middle of a decision and unsure which way is best? God is so faithful and continually states in His Word that He will direct you where you should go. Ask Him to help you make the decision. He will. Open your eyes and ears. He may speak through your pastor during his message in the worship service. He may speak through a Christian friend who may or may not know your quandary. He may even speak through a non-related book you are reading. Often He uses my daily Scripture Reading to answer my questions. The Creator of the universe is limited by nothing and loves to answer our questions.

2. When I taught Bible school in church, we told our children that God's phone number was/is Jeremiah 33:3 "Call to me and I will answer you and tell you great and unsearchable things you do not know." We want Him to tell us great and unsearchable things, don't we?! And again He promises that we can call Him and He will answer. Ask. Then look and listen.

3. After hearing Corrie ten Boom, a well-known author, speaker, and former prisoner of concentration camps during World War II, people often said, "Corrie, you have great faith!" Her response was, "No. I have faith in a great God!" We give thanks and praise to our amazing, remarkable, all-knowing, all-powerful, sovereign God!

Prayer:

Lord, I am so very grateful that You give us free will to make our own decisions while still guiding us where You want us to go. The best place for us to be is in the center of Your will. Lord, I am also thankful that You custom make our calling. Thank You for creating each of us just as You want us to be, unique. You are amazing, God! I praise You, and I pray in Jesus' wonderful, powerful name. Amen.

Added note: The day after I wrote this devotional, my Scripture for the day was Psalm 71 in which is found the proclamation that we are sheltered by our Sovereign Lord (Psalm 71:5 and 16). God often gives me confirmation that something I have written is His idea. I am so grateful. On my own, I have nothing to offer. When it's His idea, I know someone will be blessed by it! Hallelujah!

INVISIBLE

Scripture Reading: 1 Samuel 3:1-10

"Rejoice always, pray continually, give thanks in all circumstances; for this is God's will for you in Christ Jesus" (1 Thessalonians 5:16-18).

Have you ever felt invisible? I did just yesterday. There were three of us who were having a conversation, and several times when I felt that I had something to add, I would begin with two or three or even four words, only to be interrupted by one or the other of the two women. Finally, after several attempts to add to the conversation, I realized that both of these people believed that what they had to say was of more significance than what I had to add. Therefore, I silently left the area and went on to my next activity. Neither of the women acknowledged my exit. I must have been invisible to them.

At first, I felt sad and even indignant. Then I looked back to the times I tried to speak to them and decided that their not caring about my input really wasn't that important. I have many friends, including my best friend of all—my husband—who are interested in what I have to say. In fact, most of my friends are very polite and give everyone in a conversation the opportunity to speak.

Most importantly, my Lord is interested in my words every time I speak (Psalm 139:4). Anytime I converse with Him, He listens. I just need to remember to allow Him the opportunity to speak to me. I don't want to interrupt Him as I was interrupted in yesterday's conversation with the women. I want to be like Samuel in 1 Samuel 3:10 when he said, "Speak, [Lord], for your servant is listening." Jesus' body may be invisible now. But I know He is always with me. He is attune to my words, and I pray that I am attune to His.

Plan of Action:

1. When you are in a conversation with more than two people, watch that each person who exhibits the desire to add something is heard. You might say something like, "Joyce, did you want to add something?"

2. When you are in a conversation, be alert and listen to each person. Sometimes we are thinking of what we want to say instead of listening well.

3. When you are in a conversation with God, remember to listen for His voice. You won't hear Him if you are doing all of the talking.

Prayer:

Father, Jesus, and Holy Spirit, thank You for Your patience with me as You teach me to pray and hear Your voice. Please make me alert when there is someone in my group who wants to participate, but for some reason, she or he is not given the opportunity. As I walk with You in this life, I pray that I exhibit Your kindness and love. Please help me to be a gentlewoman as You are a Gentleman. Thank You, my precious Lord. I pray in Jesus' name. Amen.

JUST TURN THE PAGE!

Scripture Reading: Acts 10:9-16

"The whole Bible was given to us by inspiration from God and is useful to teach us what is true and to make us realize what is wrong in our lives; it straightens us out and helps us do what is right. It is God's way of making us well prepared at every point, fully equipped to do good to everyone" (2 Timothy 3:16-17 TLB).

One day my sister, my brother-in-law, my husband and I were discussing how I believed a particular Scripture was convicting me to do something I really didn't want to do. Because my brother-in-law agreed with me, without skipping a beat, he said, "Oh no! Just turn the page! Turn the page! There are lots of other pages in the Bible. Just turn the page!" All of us laughed! After all, that reaction was such a gut response to not wanting to do something the Lord was guiding us toward.

I must add that the four of us are Christians, and we believe the entire Bible is God's inspired Word. Yet aren't there times when we want to "just turn the page" and act like we don't know that God is leading in a certain way where we don't want to go? That's our Jonah response. You remember the story about Jonah and the whale (Jonah 1-4). Hopefully we will submit and obey God in a shorter time than it took Jonah. Or perhaps we think, "I am sure that Scripture is for that guy, but not for me."

The **Scripture Reading** is where God shows Peter a lowered sheet three times. The sheet was full of foods that Peter would never eat because, according to the Jewish faith, they were unclean. But God told him not to call unclean what He had made clean. Then we see that the reason for the vision was to open the door for Peter to go speak at a Gentile's home. God knew that without His okay, Peter would never go to a Gentile's home because it was against their law for a Jew "to associate with or visit a Gentile" (Acts 10:28).

Thankfully, we serve a gracious and loving God who is the same yesterday, today, and forever (Hebrews 13:8). Even today, and even to us, He will confirm His direction in several ways. If I am wondering if God is calling me to do something, I first try to confirm it in His Word. Then He either has a friend bring up the issue in a casual conversation, or He might have it mentioned in the worship service, or Sunday school, or Bible study, or many other ways. God is the Creator of the universe. He is not limited in ways to communicate His will to us.

Many years ago, I was blessed to attend a conference in Kansas City where Corrie ten Boom was one of the speakers. Corrie is the author of several books. The best known is *The Hiding Place*. In the middle of her message to our group, she stopped speaking, pointed to a man on the front row and said, "I don't know you, but the Lord does, and He has been speaking to you for a while about going on a designated mission. You must go." Then she resumed her original message. You see, the Lord can make His message clear in all sorts of ways.

"I will instruct you and teach you in the way you should go; I will counsel you and watch over you" (Psalm 32:8). Philippians 2:13 lets us in on one of the wonderful ways God works: "For God is working in you, giving you the desire and the power to do what pleases him" (NLT). We just need to keep our eyes open and resist the desire to "just turn the page."

Plan of Action:

1. As much as we would like to "just turn the page" and act like God isn't calling us to do something, we can't. If God is calling you to do something but you would like for him to call someone else, first confirm that it really is His call. Then obey Him and do it. Remember that He

doesn't call us to do something without equipping us to do it. "You go before me and follow me. You place your hand of blessing on my head" (Psalm 139:5 NLT).

2. Another way God uses us is in our everyday conversation. We may say something significant to someone and not even know it. Have you ever been talking, and the Lord puts a Scripture in your mind which ties into the discussion? Or maybe He reminds you of an occurrence in your life that relates to the exchange. My point here is to have your ears and eyes open as a ready vessel through whom the Lord will bless others, and you will be blessed too.

Prayer:

My Lord, I am still amazed that You use me. What an honor and privilege! Please guard my mouth that I only speak Your words, words that are bathed in love and words that show I am one of Your children. As much as I might want to "just turn the page," I desire most of all to be obedient to Your leading. Thank You again for Your living Word, the Bible, and for Christ the living Word. You have blessed me abundantly. I pray in Jesus' name. Amen.

LEADERS

Scripture Reading: 1 Kings 1:1-53

"Many are the plans in a man's heart, but it is the LORD'S purpose that prevails" (Proverbs 19:21).

"Everyone must submit himself to the governing authorities, for there is no authority except that which God has established. The authorities that exist have been established by God" (Romans 13:1).

When King David was quite old, one of his sons, Adonijah, decided to declare himself king of Israel. He made all of the preparations for the celebration, sacrificed many animals for the feast, and invited a great number of people.

One problem with Adonijah's plans and preparations was that neither his father, King David, nor God had told him that he would follow his father as king. He decided on his own to name himself king.

Once David heard that Adonijah was declaring himself king, he arranged for Zadok the priest to anoint Solomon and declare him king. Solomon was the prophet Nathan's choice. He was King David's choice. Most importantly, Solomon was God's choice. "For promotion and power come from nowhere on earth, but only from God. He promotes one and deposes another" (Psalm 75:6-7 TLB).

We can worry and fret because we don't like a particular leader, whether that is the president of the United States, or the governor of our state, or even our boss at work. Worrying is contrary to Scripture, as we see in Philippians 4:6, "Do not be anxious about anything, but in everything, by prayer and petition, with thanksgiving, present your requests to God." The Holy Spirit instructs us to pray for our leaders in 1 Timothy 2:1-2, "I urge, then, first of all, that requests, prayers, intercession and thanksgiving be made for everyone—for kings and all those in authority, that we may live peaceful and quiet lives in all godliness and holiness." We have the responsibility to vote for the leaders that we believe God wants for us, those who appear to live according to God's Word. In the end, God will allow the leader of His choice to take his leadership role, and we have the responsibility to pray for him or her.

Plan of Action:

1. Ask God to remind you to pray for our leaders on a regular basis.
2. Right now, take a few minutes to pray for our leaders.

Prayer:

Lord, please guide the leaders of our nation, our state, our city, our community, and our church. Please give them the wisdom they need to do their jobs. Help them to hear Your voice and follow Your directions. Father, please bring our country back to You. Remind me to pray for our leaders on a regular basis, and help me to remember that You chose the leaders who are in charge right now. I pray in Jesus' name. Amen.

LET US BE SALTY SALT AND SHINING LIGHTS

Scripture Reading: Psalm 19

"Let me tell you why you are here. You're here to be salt-seasoning that brings out the God-flavors of this earth. If you lose your saltiness, how will people taste godliness? You've lost your usefulness and will end up in the garbage. Here's another way to put it: You're here to be light, bringing out the God-colors in the world. God is not a secret to be kept. We're going public with this, as public as a city on a hill. If I make you light-bearers, you don't think I'm going to hide you under a bucket, do you? I'm putting you on a light stand. Now that I've put you there on a hilltop, on a light stand—shine! Keep open house; be generous with your lives. By opening up to others, you'll prompt people to open up with God, this generous Father in heaven" (Matthew 5:13-16 The Message).

Don't you love the way Eugene Peterson has written this contemporary rendering of Matthew 5:13-16? I, probably like you, am very familiar with these verses. But in Peterson's *The Message*, I get a fresh, new look at these verses.

Why does the Holy Spirit tell us through Matthew that we should be salty? We know that salt makes us thirsty. Therefore, we want to make people around us thirsty for the Lord. How do we do that? Whether in good times or bad, we seek our Lord to help us live as we should. We are quick to help those in need with God's grace. We are secure in Him, and we are willing to lavish His love on others that God places in our paths. We know that as others become thirsty for the Lord, He will quench their thirst with His presence. "If anyone is thirsty, let him come to me and drink" (John 7:37b).

Salt is also a flavor enhancer. As we submit to God's guidance, He works through us to help others taste His flavor in this world. We point out and exhibit the beauty He has created. What an honor to have God use us as flavor enhancers!

Next, the Scripture tells us we are to let God shine through us letting people know we are God's. We provide light for others to see their way to Jesus and show people the God colors in this world. "The path of the righteous is like the first gleam of dawn, shining ever brighter till the full light of day" (Proverbs 4:18). Isn't that a beautiful picture? Who doesn't want to be as beautiful as a sunrise, glowing in the magnificence of Christ?

If we have acquaintances and friends who don't know that we are Christian, we may need to allow Christ to polish up our presence so He can shine through us. Occasionally, the Holy Spirit will nudge us gently to make a statement that brings Him glory during a conversation with friends or family. The more we follow through with His nudges and speak, the easier it will be the next time, and the next. Most of the time, He just nudges, except in the case of Jonah when he resisted God's direction too many times, and he was swallowed by a whale. Don't continually resist God. You don't want to be swallowed by a whale! ☺

When our friends know we are Christian, they will know that they can come to us when they run into trouble. When we are bubbling over with gratitude for what He has done in our life, we will naturally be salt and light with our friends. It is God's job to draw them to Him. We are just the light to show them the way.

Plan of Action:

1. Are you salty salt and a shining light in your circle of friends? If one of them ran into trouble, would he or she know to depend on you for prayer and support? If so, hurrah for you and God! If not, you need to

do some serious thinking about why. In the United States, we are blessed in that we don't have to be "undercover Christians." In fact, Scripture plainly states that we are to let the world know we are Christian. Stand on that hilltop and shine!

2. If the checker at the grocery store or your hairdresser found out you are a Christian, would they be surprised? I hope not. We are to treat others with kindness serving as an example of Christ with everyone we meet. Help people taste God's goodness and see His beauty in your everyday life.

3. Are you open to God introducing you to people of His choosing who may be out of your normal circle of friends? One of my pastors made a statement recently in Sunday morning worship service that made me stop and think. "If we have no one in our lives that might cause a lifted eyebrow by our Christian friends, are we truly representing Christ in our community?" Christ loved and was open to care for all people. He did not let the views of others keep Him from loving and ministering to people out of His social circle. Consider the Samaritan woman at the well (John 4:7-42), the demon-possessed man who was so strong that no one could subdue him (Mark 5:1-20), and the woman Jesus healed of a twelve-year bleeding condition (Mark 5:25-34). These are just a few of the many people that the world looked upon as "odd" or "untouchable." Yet Jesus expressed His love by choosing to meet the needs of these social outcasts. Let's follow His example and be a blessing rather than a critic.

Prayer:

Father in heaven, please help me to be salty salt and a shining light to draw others to You. Please let my conversation always be full of grace, seasoned with salt, so I will know how to answer everyone. I do so want to shine as "the first gleam of dawn, shining ever brighter till the light of day." Help me serve You and represent You well. In Jesus' name. Amen.

"And whatever you do, in word or deed, do everything in the name of the Lord Jesus, giving thanks to God the Father through him" (Colossians 3:17 ESV).

MISPLACED EXPECTATIONS

Scripture Reading: Ephesians 2:1-10

"Ask and it will be given to you; seek and you will find; knock and the door will be opened to you. For everyone who asks receives; the one who seeks finds; and to the one who knocks, the door will be opened" (Matthew 7:7-8).

On a recent trip to Europe, my husband and I came down with very sore throats and coughs. Since we were travelers and didn't have a physician to consult, we went to a pharmacy to seek some relief. We have many pharmacy friends in the United States, and we were pretty sure that if we explained that my husband was a physician in the States and then listed our symptoms, the pharmacist could help. Sadly, she only sold us lozenges, which were worthless.

Here was our folly: we expected something of someone who was incapable of providing for our need. We should have arranged to visit a doctor who could first, diagnose, and second, send a prescription for the medication we needed to combat our germs.

We have to be careful not to have misplaced expectations of our friends and family in everyday life. We laugh about times when our children were very young, and I expected them to behave as adults. I remember calling a dear friend and sister-in-Christ and telling her that I was worried because our daughter wouldn't admit that she had sinned. My friend said, "Cheryl, think about it. She is only four years old!" That was a "come to Jesus" remark that I needed to hear for a reality check. Although our daughter was and is very intelligent, she probably didn't understand what a sin was. It was a misplaced expectation.

Years ago, I was counseling a young woman who was very angry with God, and she felt bad about it. I explained that she may as well be honest with Him about her anger because He already knew she was angry with Him and He is all powerful and strong enough to receive her anger. As I told her, God loves us and wants us to communicate with Him. We are in relationship with Him in a more intimate way than any person on earth. If we were angry with our spouse but never told him why, the anger would fester and grow. We need to discuss our feelings with our friends and family in order to keep the relationships healthy. Of course, this is the same with our Lord. Once we pour out our feelings to Him, we will feel better, and we can let Him heal our hurts. Well-placed expectation.

God can handle our expectations. He is able. He grafted us into His family (Romans 11:13-24). He loves us and wants the best for us, which may mean that His answer to our prayer may be "no" or "not now" instead of "yes." If we hurt, He will console us (Isaiah 61:1-3). If we need wisdom, He will give it (James 1:5). If we need help, He will help us (Psalm 41:1). "Let him have all your worries and cares, for he is always thinking about you and watching everything that concerns you" (1 Peter 5:7 TLB). He loves to lavish us with His favor and love.

Plan of Action:

1. Ask yourself if you have misplaced expectations of anyone. What about when you go out for dinner and you have a server who is handling you as well as another large party? You might want to extend grace to your server and adjust your expectations.

2. What kind of expectations have you placed on your daughter-in-law or your son-in-law? Do you expect them to behave exactly like your children? Extend some grace to them. They were raised in a different home with parents who raised them as they wanted to, which was probably different than your home.

3. There are lots of places where we may be placing misplaced expectations. As you go through your day, ask God to remind you not to do that, but rather to extend grace.

Prayer:

Lord, I am sure that there are people of whom I expect perfection. Yet I am not perfect! How can I expect that of others?! Pull me back. Pull me up short when I am unreasonable. You know me inside and out. Give me Your wisdom as I deal with other people. Help me to hear Your voice telling me to extend Your grace to others. Lord, I want to be Your polished ambassador. I don't want to behave in a demanding or ugly way. Let Your love flow through me in all circumstances. Thank You, Father. In Jesus' name. Amen.

NEHEMIAH
PART 1—FASTS AND PRAYS

Scripture Reading: Nehemiah 1—2:8

"If it pleases the king and if your servant has found favor in his sight, let him send me to the city in Judah where my fathers are buried so that I can rebuild it" (Nehemiah 2:5).

When Nehemiah, a cup bearer to King Artaxerxes, heard that the wall of Jerusalem was broken down, the gates burned, and the remnant of Israelites were "in great trouble and disgrace" (Nehemiah 1:3), he wept and mourned, fasted and prayed. Chapters 1-6 of Nehemiah tell of his journey with God's call on his life to rebuild Jerusalem through to its completion. This is an account of a man who was called away from his very secure, steady job to do one that by all appearances was much more physically and emotionally strenuous.

We can learn a great deal about how to approach a problem as we study Nehemiah. Verses 1-3 of Chapter 1 reveal that he searched out information about the city and well-being of his fellow Israelites. Nehemiah's response to the information he received was to weep and mourn, fast and pray (Nehemiah 1:4-11). When we receive information about others who are in need, we should ask God what we should do. Perhaps, we are to fast and pray. We may have occasion to celebrate and rejoice, or to weep and mourn. That may mean that we need to write a note, give a call, stop by a home and visit, as well as pray. God desires that we live in community . . . not on an island excluding ourselves from others. We are supposed to stay connected with other people.

In Nehemiah's prayer, we see him recognize God for whom He is. Likewise, when we remind ourselves to whom we are praying, that alone helps us keep all things in perspective. We are praying to God who made all things. There is nothing that is out of His reach. He is able even though we are not.

As Nehemiah continued to pray, he confessed the sins of his people and included his own family in that confession (Nehemiah 1:6-7). He was contrite. He placed himself in a position of showing his need for God's mercy and prepared his heart to receive whatever God had in store for him and his fellow Israelites.

In his prayer, he reminded God of His promises (Nehemiah 1:8-10). Then in verse 11, he made his request to God: "O Lord, let your ear be attentive to the prayer of this your servant and to the prayer of your servants who delight in revering your name. Give your servant success today by granting him favor in the presence of this man." Nehemiah knew he had to let King Artaxerxers know of the burden on his heart to restore Jerusalem, the home of his ancestors.

Nehemiah was a supremely trusted servant since he tested King Artaxerxes' food and drink. The king trusted him with his life. Nehemiah knew that as cup bearer he held a privileged position, and he took advantage of the place where God had put him. Furthermore, Nehemiah was willing to be transparent before the king, his employer, the person with authority (Nehemiah 2:1-3). He didn't try to keep up a controlled front, a "stiff upper lip." He let the king see that he was troubled. Notice that this demeanor was different than usual. He said that he had not been sad in the king's presence before. Does that mean that Nehemiah had never had a reason to be sad before this time? I doubt it. All of us have things that make us sad. Some are big reasons and some are small. In this case I believe that his sorrow over the state of Jerusalem was so significant that he couldn't cover it up, and he didn't try to do so.

In Chapter 2:4-8 Nehemiah told the King what he wanted. He was not timid in his request. He didn't say, "Well, King, do you suppose that I could have a little time off?" No, he told him all of his needs and wants. He had obviously thought through the situation. He serves as such a good model of the way to approach someone to request favor of some kind. He had prayed, fasted, prepared, and presented the entire need. Not only did the king send him, but he also gave him letters for timber and letters to officials to ensure safe travels.

From the moment when he first became aware of the condition of the wall of Jerusalem, Nehemiah prayed and recognized that if anything were going to change, it would be up to God. Only with God's help would King Artaxerxes release him to go restore Jerusalem. Only with God's help would they be safe. Only with God's help would they be successful. "And because the gracious hand of my God was upon me, the King granted my requests" (Nehemiah 2:8).

Plan of Action:

1. Is there a project you are about to tackle? If so, follow Nehemiah's example. Pray, fast, prepare, and if you have a superior from whom you are to receive approval, present your research.

2. Notice another practice of Nehemiah's was to constantly pray and trust that the Lord was with him on his journey. "Be joyful always; pray continually" (1 Thessalonians 5:16-17). Remember that God is the Creator and His ideas are limitless. As you live your life, ask Him for new ideas in approaching problems. When you are walking with Him and wanting His best for you, He will graciously give you fresh ideas.

Prayer:

Lord, thank You for taking care of Nehemiah and directing him as he restored Jerusalem. Thank You also for taking care of me and helping me in the different aspects of my life. With You as my Resource, I will not be limited in solving problems or creating beauty for those around me. When I have a project to complete, please help me to stay focused, be prepared, persevere, and finish the work. If I am supposed to get people to help me, let the vision of the project inspire them, and Lord, I trust that You will equip them to do the work. I thank You so very much for allowing us to read and study Your Word. Please have it sink into our souls, our minds and hearts, to change us into what You want us to be. Thank You, Lord. I pray in Jesus' name. Amen.

NEHEMIAH
PART 2—EXPERIENCES OPPOSITION

Scripture Reading: Nehemiah 2:8-20

"The king's heart is a stream of water in the hand of the LORD;
he turns it wherever he will" (Proverb 21:1 ESV).

In Nehemiah 2:8, we see that Nehemiah knew that although he was asking King Artaxerxes for permission to leave to restore Jerusalem, it was really up to God whether he would be able to go or not. " . . . And because the gracious hand of my God was upon me, the king granted my requests" (Nehemiah 2:8).

Immediately upon receiving approval from the king, Nehemiah set his feet to action (Nehemiah 2:9). He knew that God was with him in this work, and he held onto that truth through every difficulty and multiple challenges. Even though God had called him to rebuild the wall and even though He had laid the path before him, Nehemiah and his workers were continually harassed and ridiculed by Sanballat the Horonite and Tobiah the Ammonite. Nehemiah answered their insults by telling them that God would give them success (Nehemiah 2:20) and by asking Him to intervene (Nehemiah 4:4-5 and 9). He also took a proactive role by posting a guard (Nehemiah 4:9). Over and over again we see Nehemiah take his problem to the Lord in prayer and then follow his prayer with a practical method to remedy the issue at hand.

Of significance is the fact that although Nehemiah was called by God to do a work, which he bathed in prayer and gave all credit to the Lord, he was still harassed throughout the building of the wall and the gates. He was bothered by people from outside of his group and even the Jews who lived near them (Nehemiah 4:12). We tend to think that if God has called us to a work and if we keep Him at the forefront of that work, that the work will go without problems. Nehemiah shows us that is not always the case. Sometimes we will be harassed before the project begins, while the project is underway, and even after it is complete. The wonderful truth that we see in Nehemiah's experience is that God gave him discernment and wisdom every step of the way.

Plan of Action:

1. Nehemiah knew that God had called him to restore Jerusalem. When you see a project ahead of you, be sure God is calling you to do the job. If your boss has given you the project, that is enough of a confirmation that it is yours. Otherwise, check with the Lord. When you have confirmed that it is God's call, look around and choose skilled people to help you. Perhaps what you need most are prayer partners. They are always appreciated!

2. As you begin work on your project, be prepared to receive objections, criticism, and maybe even harassment. Remember that Nehemiah kept his vision focused on completing the job. He did not let himself get diverted from the task at hand. Do as he did.

Prayer:

Lord, thank You that You are always with me. You hold me in the palm of Your hand as You tell me in Isaiah 49:16. In Psalm 139:5, You promise to both precede me and follow me and lay Your hand of blessing on my head. When You give me a task, please make me strong to hold on to the vision You have given me and to persevere until I have completed it to Your satisfaction. Thank You for loving me and for instructing me. Please give me ears to hear Your directions. I pray in Jesus' name. Amen.

NEHEMIAH
PART 3—PREPARES AND PRESENTS

Scripture Reading: Nehemiah 2:11-18

"... Come, let us rebuild the wall of Jerusalem, and we will no longer be in disgrace" (Nehemiah 2:17b).

In Nehemiah 2:11, we see that Nehemiah arrived at his Jerusalem destination and stayed there for three days. During this time, he probably rested and planned his next course of action: what, how, when, where, and with whom. Generally speaking, God does not want us to work until we drop. We are at our best if we are adequately rested, allowing our Lord to refresh us. Once rested, He expects us to plan and prepare, and He graciously helps us along every step.

In the next few verses, we see that there are times to be transparent as Nehemiah was with King Artaxerxes and there are times to keep our plans secret, maintain low visibility, and quietly do our work. Not everyone needs to be apprised of our plans and activities. Nehemiah set out at night to inspect the walls and gates but told no one his plans until he knew the timing was right (Nehemiah 2:11-16). We need to follow God's direction, which we won't know if we aren't quietly listening for Him.

Also Nehemiah did his own research, and he did it at night (Nehemiah 2:13-15). He looked over the situation himself. He didn't choose necessarily the easiest or the most comfortable approach to checking out the surroundings.

He probably could have hired someone to look at the area for him. But then that person would have known his plans and might not have been trustworthy. Sometimes, the easy way is not God's way.

After he had done his homework, Nehemiah shared his vision and presented his plan to the leaders (Nehemiah 2:17-18). He included in his credentials that the hand of God was on him. Again, Nehemiah was not shy about who he was or to whom he belonged. Along with heavenly credentials, he included his earthly ones by stating that he had the approval of the king. At this point the people were convinced and ready to begin rebuilding Jerusalem.

Plan of Action:

1. Transparency is a buzzword right now in our country, and people like to say that they are exercising full transparency in their lives. However, as we learned from Nehemiah, there are times when we are not to let everyone know our thoughts and plans. Sometimes, we are to keep our thoughts to ourselves for a season and wait until the time is right to voice them. "There is a time for everything, and a season for every activity under heaven: . . . a time to be silent and a time to speak" (Ecclesiastes 3:1, 7b). When preparing for a project, wait on the Lord to give you the okay to share your plan.

2. Then as you tell others about your plan, tell them the entire vision. Sometimes we err on the side of being too brief. Nehemiah told the leaders his plan and made it plain that he had both God and human officials on his side.

Prayer:

Father, You know that I need Your wisdom in everything I do. Please help me to speak when I should and be quiet when I should. I know that in the past You have let me know information that was just for me to know in order to accomplish a work. Other times You have given me facts and knowledge that You expected me to share. Please continue to give me discernment to walk in the center of Your will. Thank You, Lord. I pray in Jesus' name. Amen.

NEHEMIAH
PART 4—HIS WORK IS CHALLENGED

Scripture Reading: Nehemiah 2:19-20; 4:1-23; 6:1-4, 15-16

"When all our enemies heard about this, all the surrounding nations were afraid and lost their self-confidence, because they realized that this work had been done with the help of our God"
(Nehemiah 6:16).

Nehemiah 2:19-20 shows us what often happens at the beginning of a new project. The opposition seizes the moment to mock, ridicule, and even try to shake the resolve of those building the walls of Jerusalem with the question, "Are you rebelling against the king?" The enemy will use any attack that he thinks might divert us from our goal. This is why we must confirm our call from God and His direction before we begin. Then we can stand on His promises. " . . . I will never leave you nor forsake you" (Joshua 1:5). " . . . The God of heaven will give us success . . . " (Nehemiah 2:20).

While much of the repairing and rebuilding of the gates was underway as recorded in Chapter 3, we find in Chapter 4 that Sanballat and Tobiah are repeating their insults and evil plots. Once again, we can learn from the spiritual and practical responses of Nehemiah's Jewish workers. They prayed and posted guards.

Notice in Nehemiah 4:12 that sometimes the enemy uses our own people to discourage us. "Then the Jews who lived near them came and told us ten times over, 'Wherever you turn, they will attack us.'" Then Nehemiah stationed families with weapons at exposed places by the wall, and he gave everyone a pep talk by reminding them with whom they fought and that they were doing this for their families' safety. He took time to give these families a vision of the plan. It is not enough to organize and send out the warriors. It is not enough to equip the warriors. We must impart the vision and remind them that God is able and God is with them. This is a good pattern for all of us.

Chapter 4:16-23 informs us that from that moment forward, one-half of the men worked on the wall while the other half held weapons and stood behind the workers protecting them. Also, every man held a weapon at his side or carried one and was ready to fight even as he worked.

We read in Chapter 6 that Nehemiah was taunted by outsiders. Sanballat and Tobiah continued to invite Nehemiah to leave the building of the wall and meet with them. Nehemiah saw the invitation for what it was: an invitation to distract the leader by pulling him away from God's call on his life. Praise God Nehemiah trusted the Lord, heard His orders, and stayed focused with his God-given discernment. When God calls, He gives whatever is needed to do His work. In this case, He not only supplied faithful workers to complete the project, He also gave Nehemiah clear discernment to separate truth from lies.

Nehemiah knew when he should listen to complaints and try to rectify the problematic situation (Nehemiah 4:11-23), and he knew when he should ignore advice offered by seemingly concerned parties (Nehemiah 6:10-13). He knew how to answer pleas for attention that were just ploys to serve as a distraction to cause him harm (Nehemiah 6:1-4). Without God's discernment, he might have been deceived.

I find it particularly interesting that his enemies continually challenged and harassed him while he faithfully did God's work. Because Nehemiah listened to God, who separated correct information from lies and who was encouraging him day by day, he was able to stay alive and out of unholy trouble. Eventually even his enemies realized "that this work had been done with the help of our God" (Nehemiah 6:16).

The book of Nehemiah illustrates that even when we are in God's will and doing what He has called us to do, sometimes we still encounter trouble and harassment. We need only be faithful to His call on our lives, pray for His discernment and direction, and keep focused on our goal. We can trust that the work will be done "with the help of our God" and to His glory.

Plan of Action:

1. Be open to hearing the Lord tell you to undertake a new project. In Matthew 9:37 the Lord tells us that the harvest is plentiful but the workers are few. As believers, God calls us to make disciples (Matthew 28:19).

2. In whatever job God has called you to do, remember that He is with you. Rely on Him to help you. He loves you and wants your work to be excellent. You are an ambassador for Christ (2 Corinthians 5:20).

Prayer:

Oh, my Lord, first of all, I thank You for Your precious Word, which You use to instruct, encourage, and enlighten. You are so gracious to love me and protect me. I do ask for Your wisdom and discernment in every part of my life. When You give me a task, help me to stay focused on it like Nehemiah, until I have it completed to Your satisfaction. I want to always give You my best. Truly, I thank You, Father—my heavenly Father, Son—my Savior and Advocate, and Holy Spirit—my Counselor and Comforter. I am so blessed to know You. Thank You for drawing me to You and removing the veil so I can know You, love You, and serve You. I pray in Jesus' Name. Amen.

OUR HOME CHURCHES

Scripture Reading: Romans 12:3-16

*"Your word is a lamp to my feet and a light for my path"
(Psalm 119:105).*

*"A new command I give you: Love one another. As I have loved
you, so you must love one another" (John 13:34).*

*"Ask and it will be given to you; seek and you will find; knock
and the door will be opened to you. For everyone who asks
receives; he who seeks finds; and to him who knocks, the door
will be opened" (Matthew 7:7-8).*

For some reason, in our fifty-three years of marriage, the Lord wanted us planted in many different communities in many different states. Consequently, numerous times we have had to go through the process of finding a new home church. First and foremost, we wanted God's Word preached without compromise. Secondly, we needed to know that the gifts God had given us could be used, and that we would be encouraged to grow in Christ. Because we have undergone the adventure of discovering His home church for us so many times, I thought you might find interesting some of our church visiting and "settling in" experiences.

One of the first churches in which He settled us was one where the pastor was so boring that we could hardly sit through the service. As we sat there, I pictured the dry bones in Ezekiel 37:1-14. We desperately needed God to put the breath of new life into the pastor's words. Every Sunday after the worship service, we would ask each other if we should look for another church. However, we were so immediately received and connected to the church members that we felt we were already part of their family. Consequently, every time we asked the Lord if we were to find another church, He reminded us of the warm, loving people in the church, and so we remained. The Lord knew, of course, that the pastor was about to receive a recommendation from the church board to retire, and so very soon, we had a new pastor through whom we were provided fresh manna.

On another of our moves, we visited several churches before we finally settled on one where we were sure we would be fed God's Word every week, and we were. As was our custom, we became involved in a Bible study group. Even with our involvement, we felt as though we were just two of many people, almost invisible, not really needed or valued. We reached out but there was no personal warmth from individuals. We had God's Word preached but no connection in true fellowship. Consequently, we began our search for another church.

In still another of our church visits, there was no doubt that we were valued and respected by the individual members as well as the pastor. We attended this church every Sunday for about two months. For each of those Sundays, the pastor seemed poorly prepared for the worship service. He would get confused as to what was next in the order of the service, and his sermons were ramblings, wandering from one subject to another. It seemed that he was adlibbing most of the sermon, which had very little substance. Finally, we recognized that the Lord was encouraging us to find another church. Leaving that church was very difficult because we had so many precious friends there. But we were not being spiritually fed, and we were so hungry for solid spiritual food that we had to move on, as God was nudging us to do.

In the next church we visited, the pastor's messages were organized, interesting, and filled with God's Word. It was apparent that he was prepared with God's help to feed his congregation with good, strong spiritual food. The worship services were orchestrated by the Holy Spirit, and we were inspired. Gratefully, we knew that we were sincerely welcomed and appreciated by the members of the church and the pastor. That became our home church for many years, and God blessed us abundantly there. We thank God for placing us in that church.

The great blessing is that God has just the right church for each person, and He will put us exactly where He knows we will be fed and can grow. " . . . He determined the times set for them and the exact places where they should live" (Acts 17:26). He directs. He provides. He blesses. And we are so grateful!

Plan of Action:

1. Pray that the pastor and other people who lead the worship service have prepared and are led by the Holy Spirit and that the Lord ministers through them to the congregation.

2. Pray for the leaders of the small groups in the church that they honor and glorify God as they lead.

3. As you prepare to go to church, pray that you will remember to think of those you will meet, and give them a warm reception.

4. If you are visiting a church to consider if it is a right fit as your home church, pray that the Holy Spirit gives you discernment about where you are to put down roots. Be sure before you visit a church that you research it to be sure it is even one you want to consider. Most churches have websites that will give you a lot of information about them.

Prayer:

Lord, please remind us to pray for the leaders of the church, the worship leaders, and especially for the pastor. Help us as members of a church congregation to warmly welcome those we meet. Teach us to love others as You love them and as You love us. We want to shed our insecurities and self-centeredness and offer a genuine love to both visitors and other members. Thank You for working through us and for continually changing us to be more like Christ. And thank You for graciously helping us find our home church. In His name I pray. Amen.

OUR PLACE IN HEAVEN

Scripture Reading: John 14:1-4

"In my Father's house are many rooms; if it were not so, I would have told you. I am going there to prepare a place for you"
(John 14:2).

Jesus tells us that He is going to prepare a place for us. Just think of it. Jesus, who created you and me, is going to prepare a place for us. But of course He is. He loves us.

If you have ever created something, you know the attachment that you feel toward it. I think of people who create quilts, all the hours that go into carefully sewing them together. It is no wonder that when they do give them away, it is usually to family or other loved ones. I have heard of painters who create beautiful paintings and find it very difficult to sell them because they have become so attached to them.

Now consider Jesus, the Master Creator, who created each of us. He loves us so much that He died (John 10:15) so that we can live with Him in heaven (John 14:3). He is preparing a place for us in Heaven where He has an inheritance waiting for us (1 Peter 1:3-4). Doesn't that bless your socks off?!

Imagine a beautiful rainbow, a magnificent sunset, an exquisite garden. Now can you imagine the place He's preparing for you? You know it will be wondrous.

Plan of Action:

1. In the next few days, pay particular attention to the beauty around you. Ask God to open your eyes to His beautiful creation including His people.

2. As you become aware of the beauty with which He has surrounded you, worship Him. Praise Him. Love Him.

Prayer:

Lord, You know that I often miss the beauty You have placed before me. Please open my eyes to see the blessings, the beauty You have surrounded me with, the wonderful things in Your Word, the world through Your eyes. Please remind me to thank You for it all. Thank You for preparing a place for me. Because You made it, I know it will be beyond what I can think or imagine. I love You, Lord. In Your name I pray. Amen.

OUR SPEECH

Scripture Reading: Ephesians 5:1-17

"Nor should there be obscenity, foolish talk or coarse joking, which are out of place, but rather thanksgiving" (Ephesians 5:4).

I want to preface this devotional by confessing that occasionally when I am surprised by a car that cuts me off on the road, or when I drop something heavy on my toe, or when I bump my head as I resume a standing position under something immovable, words come out of my mouth which do not bring glory to God. Considering I gave my life over to Him decades ago, I am sad to admit that He still has work to do with me. I think there is a bumper sticker out there that describes me: I am not perfect, but I am forgiven.

Knowing this, I want to remind myself and include you in the discussion as to why such speech is out of place in a Christian's life. I am also moved to include this subject in my book because sadly I hear Christians who use obscenities regularly out of habit. Needless to say, but I am saying it anyway, that habit needs to be broken. We are the temple of the Holy Spirit. 1 Corinthians 6:19-20: "Do you not know that your bodies are temples of the Holy Spirit, who is in you, whom you have received from God? You are not you own; you were bought at a price. Therefore honor God with your bodies."

The Holy Spirit is perfect and holy. We see this over and over in the Bible. Let's look at how Isaiah reacted when he realized he was in God's presence. "'Woe to me!' I cried. 'I am ruined! For I am a man of unclean lips, and I live among people of unclean lips, and my eyes have seen the King, the LORD Almighty'" (Isaiah 6:5). Isaiah knew immediately that he was unworthy to be in God's presence. We too are unworthy to be in God's presence. We are only made worthy because of the blood of Christ that was shed on our behalf. When we accepted Christ into our lives, the Holy Spirit made His home in us. Consequently, He hears us. Jesus our Savior also hears us. According to John 2:1 Jesus speaks to the Father on our behalf. Obviously, our Father hears us too.

With all that we do and say, we need to ask ourselves, "Does this glorify God?" 1 Corinthians 10:31 instructs us: "[W]hether you eat or drink, or whatever you do, do all to the glory of God" (ESV). I love Eugene Peterson's paraphrased translation of the fourth and fifth verses of Ephesians 5: "Though some tongues just love the taste of gossip, Christians have better uses for language than that. Don't talk dirty or silly. That kind of talk doesn't fit our style. Thanksgiving is our dialect" (*The Message*). That makes plain the way we should talk as Christians. Obscenities, dirty talk, coarse stories, even gossip are not our style as Christians who are letting God work with us to become more like Christ every day. Thanksgiving is our dialect.

Plan of Action:

1. Join me in once again giving all we are and all we have to Christ. He is worthy and holy and perfect, and He knows we are not, and yet, He still loves us. Remember Romans 5:8: "But God demonstrates his own love for us in this: While we were still sinners, Christ died for us." He loved us before we asked His forgiveness for our sinful ways, and He loves us now on our Christian journey toward eternity with Him.

2. In today's world, it is difficult to seclude ourselves from coarse talk, and when we hear it, that makes it easier to sneak into our language. One thing that we can do to fight against this is to carefully choose what we watch on the television, on our phones, and on our computers. Here is how *The Message* directs us: "So let God work his will in you. Yell a loud *no* to the Devil and watch him scamper. Say a quiet *yes* to God and he'll be there in no time. Quit dabbling in sin" (James 4:7-8 *The Message*). God loves us and loves to help us. Together let's say a quiet *yes* to God!

Prayer:

Father, thank You for not giving up on me, and thank You for loving me despite my falling short of where You want me to be. Once again, Lord, I give You all I have and all I am. Please continue to shape me and mold me into the person You know I can be. I love You, my Father, Jesus—my Savior, and Holy Spirit—my Comforter and Companion. In Jesus' name I pray. Amen.

PARENTS' LOVE FOR THEIR CHILDREN

Scripture Reading: Psalm 139:1-18

"Children are a gift from the LORD; they are a reward from him" (Psalm 127:3 NLT).

Before our first child was born, my husband and I were out for a walk, and I told him that I wasn't sure about adding to our family. I couldn't imagine that there would be enough of our love to share with a new person. What I haven't told you was that I was 8 months pregnant at the time. As you would expect, my husband wisely informed me that it was a little late to wonder about that. Of course, when Amy was born, we found that God provided an extraordinary new love for our child. He gave her to us, and He provides for all of our needs (Philippians 4:19).

Then when I was pregnant with our second child, I was concerned again that we might not have enough love to share with a new person in our family. I certainly didn't want to divide the love that we had for Amy. But God showed me that the love He gives us for our family is like a house. It is strong and steady in and of itself. Then when we decided to have a child, it was as if we added a room to our house. We didn't take away from the house that was already there. We didn't have to take half of our love from Amy. Instead, we added another room, just as God gives us extra love for both children. Subsequently, when we had our second child, God gave us additional love for him. We didn't take away from the strong and stable house with the beautiful extra room. Instead, we added still another handsome room to our house.

My love for my husband wasn't divided by three to make room for our children. Instead, God gave both my husband and me additional love for each child. I am always saddened when I hear of parents who have a "favorite" child. Have they not read the story of Jacob in Genesis 37? "Now Israel [another name for Jacob] loved Joseph more than any of his other sons" (Genesis 37:3). Because Jacob favored Joseph so much, he made him a "richly ornamented robe" for all to see. If you have read the account, you know that his brothers were jealous and decided to kill him. But they changed their minds and decided to sell him instead and show their father his bloody ornamental robe, insinuating that he had been killed by a ferocious animal. They just wanted to get rid of him.

Without question the brothers were wrong. But so was Jacob who broadcasted that Joseph was his favorite son. That caused hostility to arise in the siblings toward both the favored child and their father.

Plan of Action:

1. If you have children, ask the Lord if you show favoritism toward one over another. If so, ask Him to help you to love all of them evenly and to show your love equally to all.
2. Now is a good time to thank God for all of your children. Take a few moments to think about the good characteristics of each of your children. In the next few days, tell each child, whether young or adult, what you love about him or her.
3. If you come from a family where one or both of your parents had a favorite child, and you were not it, forgive them. Your heavenly Father makes up for the favor you didn't receive from your earthly parents.

Prayer:

Lord, thank You for my children! Please teach me to love all of them just as You created them. Help me not to show favoritism to any child, but to lavish each one with Your abundant and sincere love. I am blessed because of Your generous love for me. Please help me to spread Your love to others in my family and to people You place in my path. In Jesus' name. Amen.

PERSECUTION

Scripture Reading: Matthew 5:10-12

"Blessed are those who are persecuted for righteousness, for theirs is the kingdom of heaven" (Matthew 5:10).

I have close friends who used to have a weekly Bible study with young adults in their early twenties. Since the young adults were in school together, they saw each other often besides at the Bible study. Some of the students began to hear comments about one of the other students that were not flattering. They heard he was hateful, unkind, and made snide remarks to other students regularly. In fact, they classified him as a jerk.

Interestingly, this student came to the couple and stated that he was being persecuted because he was a Christian. After much discussion, they concluded that the other students wanted nothing to do with him, not because he was a Christian, but because he was not a nice person. Sadly, he did not receive this well and was sure that others were avoiding him because of his faith. It took several meetings for him to realize that others were avoiding him because he was not pleasant to be around.

Similarly, I remember shopping in a large furniture store. Suddenly, one of the salesmen angrily shouted, "Well, I was just trying to be a good Christian." Ummm. I don't think that is a statement that should be shouted whether angrily or otherwise. Neither Christians nor non-Christians want to hear something like that yelled.

We are called to be ambassadors for Christ in every part of our life. (2 Corinthians 5:20) When people look at us, we want them to see Christ. We want to live a life where we extend grace and mercy to others. Our lives should exhibit the fruit of the Holy Spirit: "love, joy, peace, patience, kindness, goodness, faithfulness, gentleness and self-control" (Galatians 5:22-23).

Matthew 5:10 speaks of persecution which results because we belong to Christ and follow His ways. The Apostle Paul is a perfect example of someone who was persecuted for living and speaking for Christ. In 2 Corinthians 11:24-32 we can read of his persecutions. He had been flogged, beaten with rods, and stoned. He was in danger from all different nationalities of people, including his own. He was arrested and imprisoned because he was preaching Christ.

I am sure that you have heard that there are countries where the people are not free to speak about Jesus. If they do, they may be imprisoned or just disappear, leaving their loved ones to only guess what has happened to them.

We are truly blessed in this country to be able to worship freely. We can speak about Christ without fear of imprisonment or death. Occasionally, we might make people uncomfortable, and they might shun us or say something unkind to us because they feel convicted or threatened. But rarely are we in the United States persecuted for righteousness to the degree of Apostle Paul and those countries that don't have freedom of speech.

Plan of Action:

1. Ask the Lord to prepare you to share your faith as a genuine ambassador for Christ. Be ready because He will give you an opportunity.

2. Take a few moments to pray for those in countries where Christians do not have the freedom to meet together for worship or even speak about their faith in Christ.

Prayer:

Father, thank You that I live in a country where I am allowed to go to Bible studies, worship freely, and speak about my faith to others without fear of imprisonment or worse. Lord, please protect those Christians in other countries who don't have our freedoms. And Lord, please help me to represent You well in all of my life. Please prepare me to share my faith in You. In fact, I would like to lead someone or several people to You. Help me to be ready. In Jesus' name I pray. Amen.

Side note: If you would like some help as you prepare to lead someone to Christ, you will find it in Appendix I. He is able to prepare you.

PLANS

Scripture Reading: Psalm 23

"Mortals make elaborate plans, but GOD has the last word"
(Proverb 16:1 The Message).

Many years ago, our daughter and I were talking about how the Lord was using her as a sounding board for a younger Christian woman who needed Godly wisdom and direction. Our daughter said, "Ministry opportunities don't always come when it is convenient for us." As I looked over times when we have had to alter our schedule to give someone our attention, I saw she was absolutely right. There are times when we need to adjust our schedule to allow the Holy Spirit to work through us to care for a person in need.

I am a planner. Our daughter is a planner. Our son is a planner. (My husband tolerates and balances us all.) We are happy when our plans are followed and completed. However, sometimes our plans are not His plans, and He interrupts our schedule to enable us to minister to one of His beloved people. "Many are the plans in a person's heart, but it is the LORD'S purpose that prevails" (Proverbs 19:21). Our son, our daughter, my husband, and I want God to interrupt our plans if He has something better for us to do. I am sure you agree. We always want to be in the center of His will.

Plan of Action:

1. Make your plans with a fluidity that allows God to redirect you in His way. Look at your calendar, and submit it to our Lord. Let Him alter it if necessary.

2. When someone calls you while you are in the middle of a project, ask yourself, "Do I need to set aside the project for now, and give this person my attention?" It may be a ministry opportunity that you don't want to miss. I had a friend who said, "God never does things one way. If He is using you to teach or just lend a Godly ear, He will bless you as you serve Him."

Prayer:

Almighty God, You know that I am a planner because You know all about me. I ask that You help me to easily set aside my plans if they are different than Yours. Remind me as I prepare my schedule that it may change, and if that happens, it may be You making the changes. If someone needs an arm around her, a shoulder to lean on, a person to listen as she vents, and You want to use me, help me to go where You want me to go and do Your will. I am still speechless when I realize that You actually use me as a person You work through. Please help me to be ready, Lord. Thank You for Your love. Thank You for leading me. I love You, Lord, and I pray in Jesus' name. Amen.

PRAISE THE LORD

Scripture Reading: Psalm 148

"The LORD is good to all; he has compassion on all he has made. All you have made will praise you, O LORD" (Psalm 145:9-10a).

When you read Psalm 148, did your mouth drop open when you saw the list of who and what are to praise the Lord? I love that! Everything that God made is told to praise Him, even things we don't think have a voice, like the sun and moon, the hills, the trees, snow and clouds, etc. That thrills me to picture the trees praising the Lord. I have long believed that everything that has breath is able to praise God, from a newborn kitten to a newborn child. But I didn't realize that everything, all God made, can praise Him.

I should have known because of how Jesus responded to the Pharisees when they told Him to rebuke his disciples for praising Him as He was entering Jerusalem. Jesus replied, "I tell you . . . if they keep quiet, the stones will cry out" (Luke 19:40). Before reading Psalm 148, I thought Jesus was just trying to make a point that it was right for the people to praise Him. Now I see that He meant the stones could and would cry out literally. Wow.

Psalm 148 has made me look at all that God created with new eyes. The other day after parking my car in the garage, I needed something from the trunk, and I heard a bird singing a very pretty song. I looked up and saw him in the tree by our home. He was just singing and singing. It was as though God was showing me the bird's way of praising Him. I listened for a while enjoying the concert. Then when I turned to go inside, the bird stopped singing. So I turned back around to see if he was still there. He was, and he started singing again. God gave a special concert just for me. He knew this would bless me, and so He arranged it. Truly Psalm 145:9 is true: "The Lord is good to all; he has compassion on all he has made." That includes you and me and that precious little bird.

You may be saying, "Oh come on, Cheryl Lynn. That bird was just doing what came naturally for a bird. Birds sing. How can you think that God had that bird sing just for you that day?" My answer: Because God loves me and wants to bless me, just like God loves you and wants to bless you. Open your eyes, and see how God is blessing you right now.

Just imagine when Christ returns and literally everything God created praises Jesus! "Let the heavens rejoice, let the earth be glad; let the sea resound, and all that is in it. Let the fields be jubilant, and everything in them; let all the trees of the forest sing for joy" (Psalm 96:11-12). "Let the sea resound, and everything in it, the world, and all who live in it" (Psalm 98:7). Wow! What a joyful image!

Plan of Action:

1. Spend a few minutes imagining what it will be like when Christ returns and everything that He created praises Him: the mountains, the stones, the trees, the flowers, the animals, everything that He created.

2. Now it's your turn to join the trees and the rocks to praise our Lord. You may choose to read Psalm 111, 112, 113, 138, or 144-150 to get you started. Or you may already have such a full heart that you can say, "Okay, Lord it's time for just You and me." Then take off!

Prayer:

Almighty God, thank You for continuing to teach me about this world that You created. I appreciate it much more now that I know that all You created can, will, and does praise You. What a blessing You have given me. Please continue to teach me all that You want me to learn. Open my eyes, ears, and heart to receive Your instruction. I lift my eyes and hands to You in praise. You are wondrous and awesome, loving and kind, mighty and powerful. With gratitude, I thank You. In Jesus' name. Amen.

PRAYERS

Scripture Reading: Matthew 7:7-11

"Now to him who is able to do immeasurably more than all we ask or imagine, according to his power that is at work within us, to him be glory in the church and in Christ Jesus throughout all generations, for ever and ever! Amen" (Ephesians 3:20-21).

You know that there are all kinds of prayers. Some people follow the ACTS method. That is A—<u>A</u>doration and praise of our Lord. C—We <u>C</u>onfess our sins. T—We <u>T</u>hank God for our blessings. S—stands for <u>S</u>upplication or petitioning God when we ask for something for ourselves and others.

Today I want to focus on petition: when we ask God for something specifically. I would like for you to remember the many prayers the Lord has answered for you over your lifetime. If you have not been in the habit of praying for specific things, I want you to begin today. Remember our God is our heavenly Father. He wants to bless us. He wants to let us know that He loves us.

Personally, I have found that when I pray for specifics and God answers me with specifics, my faith grows because I see Him at work in the details of my life. Decades ago when I discovered that I could pray for personal wants, we were considering looking for our first house. I wrote down everything that was important for me to have in our new home. I remember that I asked the Lord for lots of big windows because I need sunlight. I wanted three bedrooms, a basement, and a large yard—all within our budget. I also told Him that I trusted Him to provide what we needed, and if I was asking for something that He didn't want for us, He would give us something else. In fact, He led us to exactly the right home. From then on whenever we had to move, I would make a list of what I wanted and needed in a house. Then I left the results up to Him to okay or nix, and every time the Lord gave me more than I asked for. "I am the LORD your God, who teaches you what is best for you, who directs you in the way you should go" (Isaiah 48:17). He loves us, and we can trust that He places us where we are supposed to be.

Another example of Him answering my specific prayers is when our daughter was in the fourth grade. There was a little girl in the neighborhood who was very mean to our daughter. Every time the neighborhood kids would get together to play, this girl would, for no particular reason, single out our daughter and torment her. Our daughter and I prayed her behavior would change, but it didn't. Then we prayed that she would move out of the neighborhood. A few weeks later, we heard that they were moving. Do you think anything is too hard for God? "Ah, Sovereign LORD, you have made the heavens and the earth by your great power and outstretched arm. Nothing is too hard for you" (Jeremiah 32:17).

My mother told me that when I was little and she spoke too sharply to me, at night she would pray that I wouldn't remember her snippy words. I honestly don't remember her ever speaking to me in a brusque manner. I remember her as one of the kindest, sweetest, most thoughtful people that I have ever known. You see, God answered her prayers.

When my husband and I were visiting what would become our new church home, we were received warmly by a group of couples. As I started to get to know each of the people, the Lord directed me to pray for one of the women's salvation. I wrote the date down and prayed that she would open her life to accept Christ as her Savior and Lord. Months later, she told me that she hadn't been a Christian even when she was the leader of the Women's Church Association. But she had accepted Jesus as her Savior just days before, and she wanted me to know about the change in her. I told her that I had been praying for her and that I had even written down the date that I had started to pray for her. When I showed her my prayer journal, she cried . . . and I cried too. Christ built a special, sweet bond between the two of us that lasted until she graduated to heaven to be with our Lord.

I have many, many more times I could tell you about when God answered my specific prayers, but now I want you to look over your life and remember times when God answered your prayers. You might have had a problem you were trying to solve, and suddenly you thought of a solution. I love what a former television preacher once said, "If you have a great idea, just know that God gave it to you. You aren't that smart." That makes me laugh! God's Word reminds us that "Every good and perfect gift is from above, coming down from the Father of the heavenly lights . . . " (James 1:17).

Remember that sometimes God's answer to our prayer is no. He wants only what is best for us, and He will only give us what He knows is good for us. "And we know that in all things God works for the good of those who love him, who have been called according to his purpose" (Romans 8:28). Do you love God? Have you accepted Christ as your Savior? If so, then He loves you and has called you for a purpose in this lifetime and eternally. Romans 8:28 includes you. Again, He wants the best for us, His children. Jesus tells us this in Matthew 7:11: "If you, then, though you are evil [referring to our sinful nature, which we received from Adam], know how to give good gifts to your children, how much more will your Father in heaven give good gifts to those who ask him!"

Plan of Action:

1. Take some time to write down a few of your answered prayers. Perhaps you needed money, and it suddenly showed up. You may have barely escaped an accident when you cried to God for help. Or maybe you were asking for direction concerning a move in your physical location or your job. As you make your list, thank Him for loving you so much and for answering your prayers.

2. Resolve today to keep a journal with the date of your prayers and God's answers. Many times God has answered my prayers in His Word. I write

that down for when I am unsure that I am where I am supposed to be. I can go to my journal and remind myself that God led me to that place. The word "remember" is found 240 times in the Old and New Testament. God calls us to remember Him and what He does for us. "Remember the former things, those of long ago; I am God, and there is no other; I am God, and there is none like me" (Isaiah 46:9).

Prayer:

Father, how can I thank You enough for all You do for me? You created me and continue to protect, provide, lead, honor, and love me. I echo the psalmist when he said in Psalm 139, verse 6, "Such knowledge is too wonderful for me, too lofty for me to attain." Thank You, Lord. Please constantly remind me to thank You. I always want to see You at work in my life and to express my awe and gratitude. You are amazing and wonderful! I love You, Lord, and I pray in Jesus' name. Amen.

PRIDE AND HUMILITY

Scripture Reading: Philippians 2:5-8

"And being found in appearance as a man, he humbled himself by becoming obedient to death—even death on a cross!"
(Philippians 2:8)

When my husband and I were on a tour of a city in Germany, we were informed by the tour guide that many years ago there was a competition between the bishop of this particular town and the archbishop of another city. Because the bishop was close friends with the pope of that time, and the bishop didn't like the archbishop to whom he was supposed to submit, the pope allowed the bishop to change the look of the cross that was above his church. Instead of just the one horizontal line going through the vertical line of the cross, the bishop could put another horizontal line. So there was the one vertical line with two horizontal lines, and this was to signify that the bishop didn't have to answer to the archbishop. The bishop only had to answer to the pope.

It struck me how human beings, even church leaders, had taken the humble sign of the cross, where our Lord God humbled Himself to die on that cross, and they used it as a sign of pride of one person over another. I picture God just shaking His head. As Romans 3:23 states, "[A]ll have sinned and fall short of the glory of God," even church leaders. One of the pastors we listen to on the radio continually reminds us that at best we are men and women, and we are men and women at best. In other words, as long as we are dealing with human beings, we are dealing with imperfect people, sinners. We hope as Christians that we are on a continual quest to become more like Christ every day. Nevertheless, we are still sinners, whether a pope, a pastor, or a church attendee . . . we are humans, and we are prone to sin.

Plan of Action:

1. There is no doubt as we read the Scriptures that God wants us to be humble. Ask Him if there is someplace in your life where you have arrogance or pride? Quietly wait and watch for His finger to point to that place. Shift your attitude from being proud of yourself for that achievement to realizing that you have achieved that because God has blessed you with the ability for that.

2. Psalm 25:9 "He guides the humble in what is right and teaches them his way." We want to be teachable; we especially want to learn what God wants us to know. To be teachable is to admit that there are things and ways we do not know. Then we can come to God and ask Him to teach us.

Prayer:

Lord, I admit that there are so many things that I do not know. I am sorry for the times that I have taken credit for achievements in my life that wouldn't have happened without You. Help me never to have a haughty, arrogant attitude. Without You I can do nothing. I do know that, Lord. I trust You to teach me what I need to know and to point out anytime I let pride sneak into my thinking. In Jesus' name I pray. Amen.

REFLECT HIM

Scripture Reading: Exodus 34:29-35

"And we all, with unveiled faces all reflect the Lord's glory, are being transformed into his likeness with ever-increasing glory, which comes from the Lord, who is the Spirit"
(2 Corinthians 3:18).

Have you noticed how just one drop of water reflects the light? The other day while I was waiting for my English muffin to toast, I looked at the floor and wondered if someone had dropped glitter on the floor. But no, I had just washed my hands, and obviously, water dropped from my hands before I dried them.

One drop of water, all by itself, was reflecting the light enough to get my attention. 2 Corinthians 3:18 says, "And we, who with unveiled faces all reflect the Lord's glory, are being transformed into his likeness with ever-increasing glory, which comes from the Lord, who is the Spirit." I can and should reflect the Lord's glory enough to draw attention to Him. How do I do that? I just let God beam through me. I don't have to yell or jump up and down. I don't have to shove or push. I just let Him reflect His glory through me. Of course, it is true that the better I know Him, the better I will reflect Him. And the more I read His Word, the more I will know Him.

Years ago, after I had spent a great deal of time studying God's Word one morning, I left the house to go to a meeting, and one of my neighbors said, "Oh my, Cheryl, you are glowing." I want you to know that was all God, not Cheryl.

Plan of Action:

1. If you are not already doing so, decide today to spend time everyday reading God's Word. I read somewhere that the Bible is the only book you read with the author right there with you. He wants us to know Him and to know and understand His Word.

2. Think about your conversations. Have you fallen into some bad habits? Your speech should reflect Him. That means no gossip, no off-color stories, no foul language.

3. What about your choice of clothing? Does it reflect the purity of Christ? Would you be embarrassed if as you turned a corner, you came face to face to Jesus?

4. Does your home reflect your faith? It needs to be welcoming and somewhat orderly, always ready to welcome someone who has come to visit. It doesn't need to be the latest in décor. In fact, when people need to be ministered to, they are not going to notice your décor. Just give them a comfortable place to sit.

Prayer:

Lord, let us be as mirrors, brightly reflecting Your glory. Please let all that I have and all that I am reflect Your loving kindness and purity. I know that You will prepare me to help anyone You place in my path who needs You and Your help. Take away any timidity or anxiousness. Don't let me be self-conscious. Instead let me think only of how You are going to minister through me. You are wonderful and amazing, Lord. I love You, and I pray in Jesus' name. Amen.

REMEMBERING

Scripture Reading: Deuteronomy 8:1-18

"[T]he Lord Jesus on the night when he was betrayed took bread, and when he had given thanks, he broke it, and said, 'This is my body, which is for you. Do this in remembrance of me.' In the same way also he took the cup, after supper, saying, 'This cup is the new covenant in my blood. Do this, as often as you drink it, in remembrance of me'" (1 Corinthians 11:23b-25 ESV).

God is big on remembering. Multiple Scriptures tell us to remember certain promises or events. God tells the Israelites to remember who brought them out of Egypt (Deuteronomy 6:12). He instructs them to teach their children about the meaning of the decrees and laws that God gave them (Deuteronomy 6:20-25). Deuteronomy 32:7 says, "Remember the days of old; consider the years of many generations; ask your father, and he will show you, your elders, and they will tell you" (ESV).

He told us that when we see the rainbow, that is His sign of His covenant between Him and all living creatures to never again destroy all life by a flood (Genesis 9:12-17). God remembered the covenant with Abraham, Isaac, and Jacob when Israelites were groaning in slavery under the Egyptians (Exodus 2:23-25). God tells us in Isaiah 49:15-16 that He will not forget us. In fact, in Isaiah 49:16 we find that He has inscribed us on the palms of His hands.

As I said, God is big on remembering. He remembers His promises to us, and He wants us to remember what He has taught us in the past and what we learn from His Word presently. Jesus told us in John 14:26 that our heavenly Father gives us the Holy Spirit to teach us and to remind us of what Jesus said.

Plan of Action:

1. The next time you are with an elderly relative, elderly friend, or elderly neighbor, listen to them patiently as they recount things of long ago. Your attention will bless them, and you just might learn something that you didn't know.

2. Those of us who live in America are blessed to have multiple versions of the Bible available to us. We are able to read in God's Word about His covenants, His miracles, and His instructions. If you don't presently have a daily plan to help you read the Bible, there are many out there for you to use. I use *The Daily Bible Reading Guide* from the American Bible Society. Go to their website, and click on Resources. Click on Daily Bible Reading, and scroll to the bottom of the page. Under Downloads, click on Daily Bible Reading PDF, then press print. Since there are two sides, click on Properties on your computer, and choose "Print on both sides." Press print, and there you go!

Prayer:

Lord, thank You for allowing me to live in a time when Your Word is available to read whenever I want to. Thank You for the many resources we have to aid in our study of the Bible. I am also grateful for the Holy Spirit who helps me to understand Your Word. Wash us with Your Word, dear Father, Son, and Holy Spirit. In Jesus' name I pray. Amen.

RIGHTEOUS

Scripture Reading: 1 John 1:7-10

"If we confess our sins, he is faithful and just and will forgive us our sins and purify us from all unrighteousness" (1 John 1:9).

What does it mean to be righteous? It means that we are made right with God. It means that God can look at us as pure, sinless. Yet we know from Romans 3:23 that we have all sinned. Therefore, on our own, we are unrighteous. We are sinful by our very nature. It is written in Psalm 14:2-3: "The LORD looks down from heaven on the sons of men to see if there are any who understand, any who seek God. All have turned aside, they have together become corrupt; there is no one who does good, not even one."

So how do we become righteous? First, we accept Christ as our Savior, which means we accept that His death was the sacrifice made in exchange for the death we deserve because we are sinful. "[F]or all have sinned and fall short of the glory of God" (Romans 3:23). Then we sincerely confess those sins to God, and He cleanses us from all unrighteousness (1 John 1:9). Just that simple. Not because we deserve it, but because He loves us. "God made him [Jesus] who had no sin to be sin for us, so that in him we might become the righteousness of God" (2 Corinthians 5:21). As a child when we fell in the mud, or even when our fingers became sticky from food, either we or our parents washed off the mud or food. Then we were clean. When we sin, we come to Jesus and ask Him to wash off the sin, and God removes it "as far as the east is from the west" (Psalm 103:12). Then we are clean—righteous.

Why do we want to become righteous? First of all, we want to be righteous because only then can we enter the Kingdom of God. Thank God we have an Intercessor who is speaking to God on our behalf if we have accepted Christ as our Savior. That Intercessor is Christ. "Who is he that condemns? Christ Jesus who died—more than that , who was raised to life—is at the right hand of God and is also interceding for us" (Romans 8:34). Furthermore, 1 Peter 3:12 says "For the eyes of the Lord are on the righteous and his ears are attentive to their prayer, . . . " I want the eyes of the Lord on me, and I want Him to hear my prayers. ". . . The prayer of a righteous man is powerful and effective" (James 5:16). I want my prayers to be powerful and effective. Don't you? Jesus tells us in Matthew 6:33: "But seek first his kingdom and his righteousness, and all these things will be given to you as well." Just previous to this verse, He was telling us not to worry about what to eat or wear because He will provide what you need. We can be encouraged by Matthew 5:6: "Blessed are those who hunger and thirst for righteousness, for they shall be satisfied" (NAS). We want to be righteous, and God says that if we fervently seek righteousness, we will be satisfied. He wants us to be righteous too. We serve a loving and generous God!

Can we make ourselves righteous by doing good to others, by giving money or property to charities, by joining a certain church, by praying "The Lord's Prayer" over and over, or by mowing the neighbor's lawn? No. We cannot earn or buy righteousness. The Apostle Paul informs us in Ephesians 2:8-9, "For it is by grace you have been saved, through faith—and this not from yourselves, it is the gift of God—not by works, so that no one can boast." As you read earlier, we are only made righteous by accepting the fact that Jesus gave Himself to die on the cross in place of us. Because of our sin, we should die. "For the wages of sin is death, but the gift of God is eternal life in Christ Jesus our Lord" (Romans 6:23). But Jesus took our sin on Him, and He died in our place. He is the only way we can get into our heavenly Father's presence. "Jesus answered, 'I am the way and the truth and the life. No one comes to the Father except through me'" (John 14:6). Jesus is now at the Father's right side speaking on our behalf. He is Jesus Christ, the Righteous One (1 John 2:1).

Then why do we as believers in Jesus give to charities and help people? We do good works because God wants us to. "For we are God's workmanship, created in Christ Jesus to do good works, which God prepared in advance for us to do" (Ephesians 2:10). Because the Holy Spirit lives in us, we find that we want to do good for others. God loves all people, and because He lives in us, we love others. He has given us a new life, a new perspective. We want to please Him. Not so He'll save us and take us to Him, but because He already promised He'd do that when we accepted Christ as our Savior. We see that in Titus 3:4-7. "But when the kindness and love of God our Savior appeared, he saved us, not because of righteous things we had done, but because of his mercy. He saved us through the washing of rebirth and renewal by the Holy Spirit, whom he poured out on us generously through Jesus Christ our Savior, so that, having been justified by his grace, we might become heirs having the hope of eternal life."

This is just a small reminder of who we are in Christ.

Plan of Action:

1. Ask yourself if there is someone in your life who has not accepted Christ as his or her Savior. Ask God for the opportunity to share Him with that person. Then wait for His nudge. Here are some instructions you might find helpful as you share Christ's saving grace with someone. (I have made the person masculine just to make the instructions less cumbersome.)

    a. He needs to admit that he has sinned and sincerely confess those sins to God.

    b. He should state that Jesus is Lord and believe in his heart that God raised Him from the dead (which you will find in Mark16:6). Then, he will be saved.

    c. Now that he is a child of God (John 1:12), encourage him to find a good, Bible-preaching church where he can be nourished by God's Word in Christian fellowship. Also encourage him to get involved in a Bible study where he can grow in the knowledge of the One who created him and who loves him very much.

    d. You and he can rest in Philippians 1:6 "[B]eing confident of this, that he who began a good work in you will carry it on to completion until the day of Christ Jesus." He is in His capable hands.

2. This is a good time to remind ourselves that we are saved only by His grace and not because of anything we have done nor because we deserve it. He chose us while we were yet sinners and died for us (Romans 5:8). He chose us and died for us because of His grace and unending love.

Prayer:

Lord, how can I thank You for my eternal life with You? I don't know why You died for me, Jesus, but I am eternally grateful and humble to accept Your precious sacrifice on my behalf. I ask, Lord, that You help me to grow in faith, in the knowledge of Your Word, in understanding of who You are, and please help me to grow to be more and more like Christ. And, Lord, please help me to share Your saving grace with others You place in my path. Open my eyes to see those in need of Your love and new life. Thank You, my heavenly Father. I pray in Jesus' name. Amen.

THE "RIGHT" WAY

Scripture Reading: Philippians 2:3-11

"Do all things without grumbling or disputing, that you may be blameless and innocent, children of God without blemish in the midst of a crooked and twisted generation, among whom you shine as lights in the world, . . . " (Philippians 2:14-15 ESV).

I was recently in a meeting where the leaders stumbled through the substance of the meeting with parliamentary corrections and "replays." It was obvious to anyone who knew parliamentary procedures that things were not being carried out according to *Robert's Rules of Order*. Nevertheless, for those of us who knew the heart of the organization and the hearts of those actively involved in the group, the "right" way was not as important as accomplishing the tasks at hand. In addition, we esteemed the wonderful giftedness of the individual leaders rather than focusing on their mistakes, which were insignificant for this meeting.

I overheard a grumbler behind me who corrected each misstep or offered an editorial opinion as issues were stated, amended, and voted on. Interestingly, "the knowledgeable one" would only speak loud enough for those seated right by him to hear. In other words, his remarks were to let us know that he knew how things should have gone, deeming those in charge not as intelligent as him.

As the meeting proceeded, we eventually found that this all knowledgeable one was at this meeting to receive a monetary scholarship from the very group whom he had continuously criticized. Instead of an attitude of humility and gratefulness, he had a smug, critical attitude of superiority and disdain. I have no doubt that if the leaders knew of his attitude before deciding who would receive the scholarship, it would have been awarded to someone else.

Plan of Action

1. Ask yourself if you exhibit an attitude of gratefulness or one of superiority. In Philippians 2:3 in the *New Living Translation* of the Bible, the apostle Paul instructs us, "Don't be selfish; don't try to impress others. Be humble, thinking of others as better than yourselves."

2. If there is a time when you find yourself unduly critical, confess that to God, who is gracious and eager to forgive you. Then ask Him to help you to slough off the critical attitude and to replace it with one of gratefulness and love. Remember the saying is true that no one cares how much you know until they know how much you care.

Prayer

Lord, we know that it is always easier to complain than encourage and help. Please forgive us for the times that we consider ourselves better than others. You instruct us in Philippians 2:5-7, "Your attitude should be the same as that of Christ Jesus: who, being in a very nature God, did not consider equality with God something to be grasped, but made himself as nothing, taking the very nature of a servant, being made in human likeness." Father, please help us to remember that we are to serve others and not expect others to serve us. We are grateful that this is Your will for us. We place ourselves before You, allowing Your Holy Spirit to make us more like Christ. In Jesus' name. Amen.

SAY "THANK YOU"

Scripture Reading: Luke 17:11-19

"And whatever you do, whether in word or deed, do it all in the name of the Lord Jesus, giving thanks to God the Father through him" (Colossians 3:17).

"Therefore encourage one another and build each other up, . . . "
(1 Thessalonians 5:11).

In the **Scripture Reading** above, you read about Jesus healing the ten lepers, and only one came back to thank Him. In Luke 17:17-18, we read, "Jesus asked, 'Were not all ten cleansed? Where are the other nine? Was no one found to return and give praise to God except this foreigner [a Samaritan]?'"

When I read that story as a child, it made a deep impression on me. I asked the Lord to help me always to show my gratitude. I did not/do not want to be like the other nine lepers who didn't return to thank and praise God for what He had done for them. As I have grown spiritually and studied God's Word, I have found there are many Scriptures that direct us to thank God for our lives, His provision, His love, and our salvation. We are also to thank, lift up, and encourage people around us for their part in our lives.

First let's thank God. Deuteronomy 8:18 states, "But remember the LORD your God, for it is he who gives you the ability to produce wealth, and so confirms his covenant, which he swore to your forefathers, as it is today."

Whatever we have today, we have it because God gave it to us. Someone might say, "But I went to college and studied hard to prepare for the position I have today." Who created the brain that enabled you to study in college? Right! God did.

On January 23, 2022, Trent Casto, the senior pastor of Covenant Church in Naples, Florida, conveyed this encouragement to his congregation, "Giving thanks to God for our blessings is one way we keep our blessings from becoming our gods. We worship the Giver of the gifts. We don't worship the gifts. In fact, we wouldn't have life without God. He gives us our very breath." "This is what God the LORD says—he who created the heavens and stretched them out, who spread out the earth and all that comes out of it, who gives breath to its people, and life to those who walk on it: I the LORD, have called you to righteousness; I will take hold of your hand" (Isaiah 42:5-6a). In Acts 17:25b we read, " . . . he himself gives all men life and breath and everything else." Lord, I thank You for every breath and for everything else.

Our generous God knows that we all need encouragement in life. Look at His Words of encouragement in Psalm 31:24: "Be strong and take heart, all you who hope in the Lord." Then Joshua reminds us of God's promise in chapter 1 verse 9: "Have I not commanded you? Be strong and courageous. Do not be afraid; do not be discouraged, for the LORD your God will be with you wherever you go." In Psalm 10:17 it is written, "You hear, O LORD, hear the desire of the afflicted, you encourage them, and you listen to their cry." God reminds us in Psalm 121:1-2 where our help comes from: "I lift my eyes to the mountains—where does my help come from? My help comes from the Lord, the Maker of heaven and earth."

There are people in your life who also need to be thanked and encouraged. What about your pastor, a mentor, a small group leader, a former teacher, a special friend—present or past? The list is as long as your memory of people who helped you in some way with their gift of knowledge, wisdom, or encouragement. It would be a wonderful blessing to them if you would take a few minutes and write them a note of appreciation for their hard work, insight, etc. Also remember to praise the Lord for their influence in your life. It is awesome to know that God orders every part of our life, and He placed those people there to help you.

Not only do we need to express appreciation to our leaders, but leaders also need to show their appreciation to their group members. They can do something as simple as thanking them for attending. If they know someone is new, they can ask where they are from or how their week was. Showing some kind of real interest in the individual makes a big difference in how a person feels when attending a new group.

During discussion in Sunday school or Bible study, the leader can say something like, "I hadn't thought about that. That gives me a different perspective." Or "That is a really good point. I will remember that." Of course, with each question or statement, the speaker must look at the person and really listen to his or her answer. How many times have we spoken with someone only to have their eyes roaming all of the time that we are responding to a question they had asked, leaving us to wonder if they really care what we are saying?

Let me finish with two more Scriptures. "And let us consider how we may spur one another on toward love and good deeds. Let us not give up meeting together, as some are in the habit of doing, but let us encourage one another—and all the more as you see the Day approaching" (Hebrews 10:24-25). And "Do not let any unwholesome talk come out of your mouths, but only what is helpful for building others up according to their needs, that it may benefit those who listen" (Ephesians 4:29). No matter what our role in life, we need to express gratitude and encourage others.

Plan of Action:

1. Sit down today and write a note of appreciation to two people you thought of while reading this devotional.

2. Now make a list of at least two more people who have helped you in some way. You may want to call them or ask them to lunch and tell them how much they mean to you.

3. Decide now to be quick to write "thank you" notes to people when they give you a gift. Don't look at this as a duty. Instead look at what a blessing it will be for the gift giver. It is a ministry opportunity. Ask the Lord to help you, and He will.

Prayer:

Lord, please remind me to always thank You for everything every day. Help me to have a heart of gratitude toward You and to others. I desire to be an instrument of Yours to encourage others in their walk with You and in the daily needs in their lives. In everything that I do, Lord, use me as a vessel of Yours for whatever blessings You want to bestow. I do love You so very much. I pray in Jesus' name. Amen.

SIMEON

Scripture Reading: Luke 2: 21-35

"Sovereign Lord, as you have promised, you may now dismiss your servant in peace. For my eyes have seen your salvation, which you have prepared in the sight of all nations, a light for revelation to the Gentiles, and the glory of your people Israel"
(Luke 2:29-32).

Can you imagine if you were Jesus' parents? You take your baby Son, who is just a few weeks old, to Jerusalem to consecrate Him to God and to offer a sacrifice as is required in the Law of the Lord. While there, an elderly gentleman walks up to you, takes your child in his arms, and thanks God for allowing him to see the Messiah before he died. Simeon blessed Joseph and Mary and then prophesied over Mary.

The Lord had promised Simeon that he would not die before he would see Christ the Messiah. Verse 25 of Luke 2 states, "the Holy Spirit was upon him." Make note, the Holy Spirit was not upon everyone at this time. But from what we read in the Bible about Simeon, he was in touch and in tune with the Lord God. On this particular day in time, Simeon was moved by the Holy Spirit to go to the temple where he found Joseph, Mary, and Jesus. What a joy for Simeon!

Of course, Joseph and Mary already knew Jesus was/is the Christ. But what a wonderful encouragement and touch from the Lord confirming again that baby Jesus is the Christ. "And Joseph and His mother marveled at those things which were spoken of Him" (Luke 2:33 NKJV).

Have you had a time in your life when you knew God was leading you to do something, and as you obeyed, you recognized God's hand in your life? Didn't you marvel at God's touch? The Bible says that Simeon was righteous and devout. We are righteous because of the shed blood of Christ (2 Corinthians 5:21). We have the Holy Spirit in us because we have accepted Christ as our Savior and we have asked for the Holy Spirit (Acts 2:38 and Luke 11:13). I pray we are devout. I want us always to be in touch and in tune with our God.

Plan of Action:

As you go through the day, look for opportunities to bless people who cross your path. I don't, however, suggest that you take someone's baby in you arms unless you know them. I am suggesting that you keep aware of those around you to whom you can say a kind word, give a warm smile, or offer a kindness. Be creative, and let God lead you.

Prayer:

Father, I think of the joy Joseph and Mary felt when Simeon took Jesus into his arms and gave thanks to You that he was indeed able to see the Messiah before he died. How wonderful for him and for Joseph and Mary. I believe that we have opportunities in our lives where we too can bless others. Open our eyes to see those You want to bless, and then help us to act obediently. You are such a wonderful God. I am so grateful to have You as my Father, Jesus as my Lord and Savior, and the Holy Spirit as my Comforter and Teacher. In Jesus' precious name I pray. Amen.

SITTING ON THE OUTSIDE, BUT DANCING ON THE INSIDE

Scripture Reading: Psalm 150

"Let them praise his name with dancing and make music to him with tambourine and harp" (Psalm 149:3).

After all of the ladies in our Circle—a fellowship group in our church—had greeted one another and rejoiced in seeing each other, I knew I was expected to settle down and sit in my chair, but I felt like dancing before the Lord. It was such a joyous occasion, and there was so much love and joy in that room. Nevertheless, I did sit down on the outside, but I smiled as I danced with the Lord on the inside in my mind.

I experienced a similar feeling when my husband and I visited a very staid, regimented worship service. Everything in the service was planned and printed in the bulletin, and yet the service was lovely. It is just that I had the feeling that I wanted to stand up and praise God by smiling at Him, raising my hands in adoration, and even dancing before Him. I am so reserved that I wouldn't have danced in front of others even if there had been others in the service who did. I just know that I wanted to do it. The Holy Spirit was dancing within me. Isn't that a great visual?

There are many occurrences in the Bible where people rejoiced and danced before the Lord. One of the most well known is when David danced before the Lord in 2 Samuel 6:14. When the Lord saved the Israelites from

Pharaoh's army, "... Miriam the prophetess, Aaron's sister, took a tambourine in her hand, and all the women followed her, with tambourines and dancing" (Exodus 15:20), as they sang praises to God.

When I am home alone, and no one is around, I do dance before the Lord as I praise Him and thank Him for His loving me. I am not yet brave enough to dance in praise in front of other people. But I know He is blessed when we praise Him with our whole being, the being that He created. With every part of me, I praise the LORD!

Plan of Action:

1. Ask the Lord to teach you how to worship him, and listen for Him to answer your prayer, either today or in the future. You ask. He will answer.

2. Rejoice in the different ways we can worship: singing, clapping, raising our hands, and yes, even dancing.

Prayer:

Lord, thank You so much for sending the Holy Spirit who teaches us how to praise You! I pray that I honor You with the praise that You deserve, in the way You deserve. Please continue to teach me to praise You with my whole being, focused on only You. Thank You for Your love, and thank You for creating me for Your glory. I pray in Jesus' name. Amen.

SOUVENIRS

Scripture Reading: Ecclesiastes 4:9-12 and 1 Peter 4:8-10

"For in him all things were created: things in heaven and on earth, visible and invisible, whether thrones or powers or rulers or authorities; all things have been created through and for him"
(Colossians 1:16).

After spending seventeen days on a European river cruise, I was thinking of the souvenirs that we brought home: a pretty bracelet from Regensburg, Germany; chocolates from Vienna, Austria; a lovely mug from Bratislava, Slovakia. I am very pleased with our purchases, yet I find that my most treasured souvenirs were not purchased. They are my memories of the people we were blessed to get to know both on our ship and even the guides from the different countries we visited. Amazingly, I believe we made some of what will prove to be lifelong friends. On our ship, we had an Austrian, a Ukrainian, Canadians, Australians, people from New Zealand and the United Kingdom, and those of us from the United States. I think of our new friends every day and wonder how they are. I am surprised and blessed that I think of them as warmly as I do some friends we have had for years.

Isn't it wonderful when God brings new friends into our lives? This gathering was particularly fun because there were so many different accents. There was this one couple from Australia with whom, almost from our first meeting, we felt a close connection. Then there was a couple from the United Kingdom. The gentleman was quick to make us laugh, and we could easily tell that his wife enjoyed his humor as much as we did. I have wondered how they reacted to the death of their Queen. I could list specific personality traits of each of the different people who were with us on our cruise because throughout the trip we moved from one group to another and enjoyed becoming acquainted with new people. Although we started the cruise as strangers, we ended as friends. My husband and I take this as a special gift from God for all of us, and we cherish it.

Plan of Action:

1. Psalm 145:9 states: "The LORD is good to all; he has compassion on all he has made." Since all people are important to God, they should be important to us too. Therefore, when God blesses you, allowing you to travel to another city, state, or even country, I suggest that you make a point to reach out and meet new people. Ask pertinent questions like where they are from, do they have children, grandchildren, what do they do for a living, is this their first trip to the state or country? You get the idea. Find out who they are. Generally speaking, people like to talk about themselves.

2. When you have asked others about their lives, be ready to answer their questions about your life. It should be an easy back and forth conversation.

3. Don't disregard those people who are sitting at a table next to you. When we were at a restaurant in Cologne, Germany, we heard the girls next to us speaking English. We found out they were from Ireland, and they were as interested in our travel experiences as we were in theirs. The entire meal was such a treat because while we ate our authentic Jaegerschnitzel, we had a lovely conversation with the Irish girls.

4. Another group of people you shouldn't disregard are those who serve you, literally the waiters and waitresses. If you are in a country that speaks a language that you aren't familiar with, getting to know your servers might be tricky. We have found that sign language works sometimes.

We also have asked Google to translate an English question or statement into German. That works very well, and usually causes a smile on the server's face.

5. Before traveling to a country where the people speak a language you don't know, use a language app to learn a few words: please, thank you, yes, no, where is the bathroom/toilet ☺. Most of the time, the people of the other country will appreciate your effort. I have found this so in Austria, France, Germany, Holland, Hungary, and even in our local Mexican restaurant where our servers are from Mexico.

Prayer:

Father, please remind me that I am one of Your ambassadors whether I am shopping at my local grocery store or traveling in a foreign country. You created every person I know and every person I meet. I know this in my head, but as I consider all of the countries, all of the different languages, I am naturally in awe that You know if a hair falls from one of our heads. Thank You for loving us. Please help me to represent You well. I am grateful for Jesus, and I pray in His name. Amen.

"For God so loved the world that he gave his one and only Son, that whoever believes in him shall not perish but have eternal life," (John 3:16).

A SURE FOUNDATION

Scripture Reading: Matthew 7:24-27

"Everyone then who hears these words of mine and does them will be like a wise man who built his house on the rock"
(Matthew 7:24 ESV).

As I have grown older, I find that when I want to underline something in a book, I need to use a straightedge because my freehand underlining has become shaky. I have also discovered that the straightedge is only good if it is made of a very solid material in order to withstand the pressure of my pen. Isn't that true of our faith and God's grace? Jesus said in Matthew 17:20, " . . . Truly I tell you, if you have faith as small as a mustard seed, you can say to this mountain, 'Move from here to there,' and it will move. Nothing will be impossible for you." Then we read in Ephesians 2:8-9 "For it is by grace you have been saved, through faith—and this is not from yourselves, It is a gift from God—not by works, so that no one can boast." God loves to give us whatever we need in order to follow Him more closely and obediently. We don't want our faith to be shaky. If we need faith, we just need to ask Him, and He will give it to us because He loves us.

Another observation I have made recently is that if I am underlining a sentence and the book is atop several other items, it tends to shift under the weight of my hand. The result is a jagged underline, not unlike if I hadn't used a straightedge at all. This reflects our lives if we place our value on money or material goods or fame or power or even other people. If we look for fulfillment anywhere besides Christ, our lives will continually shift toward the next accomplishment or material object.

I am sure we all have friends who are seeking happiness in the next purchase. Then, once they have that, they are on to their next purchase to make them happy. We know that trying to find fulfillment in anyone or anything other than Christ is not going to happen. They can continue to buy and buy and buy until they have no more money, and they will never find the peace and joy they are looking for until they receive the Prince of Peace, the Giver of joy, the Creator of all people and all things—Jesus.

Plan of Action:

1. Let your mind bring to you a person or people who are not believers, who are seeking joy and fulfillment in something or someone besides Jesus. Ask the Lord to draw them to Him and bless them with the saving knowledge of Jesus.

2. Knowing that we are to pray constantly (1 Thessalonians 5:17), ask the Lord to remind you to pray for those who cross your paths throughout the day and who need Him.

Prayer:

Father, I thank You for the peace You give Your children. I am grateful that I can say with Your help, I have learned to be content whatever the circumstances. Please open my eyes and give me discernment as I go through my days and interact with others. Let me see those in need of You and move me to pray for them. If You want me to introduce them to You, I ask that You make that very plain to me and that You give me the words and the courage. You are a wonderful God and Father. I love You, Lord. In Jesus' name. Amen.

TAKE THE HEADLINES TO THE PRAYER CLOSET

Scripture Reading: Luke 11:9-13

"Do not be anxious about anything, but in everything, by prayer and petition, with thanksgiving, present your requests to God" (Philippians 4:6).

"I urge, then, first of all, that requests, prayers, intercession and thanksgiving be made for everyone—" (1 Timothy 2:1).

Have you noticed the headlines lately? What about when Julia Roberts is interviewed? Or when there is another report about some activity of the Kardashians? What is new with the royals in England and Prince Harry and Meghan? How do you react when President Biden or former President Trump has a press conference? These people have the blessing or curse of being famous, and therefore, we have the curse or blessing of hearing about their behavior. Let's make it a blessing by taking them before the Lord in prayer and asking for His intervention on their behalf to draw them to Him.

As believers who walk in grace, I believe one of our responsibilities is to be alert to those who don't know Him and pray that they yield to the Holy Spirit's leading so they can come to know Him. I don't know if Julia Roberts, the Kardashians, the royals, President Biden, or former President Trump are believers, but I pray that God draws them close to Him and leads them into a personal relationship with Him.

What was your reaction when you heard that Alex Trebek died? Did you think to pray for his family, friends, and even the Jeopardy organization? Have you thought to pray for the sports figures who are constantly in the news?

How do you feel about immigration? The deficit? Our country's leaders, their counselors and staff? Our schools? The violence that is erupting on airplanes? The point is that as we listen to or read these headlines, they are opportunities for prayer. If something we see or hear stirs a reaction in us, take that as a cue from the Holy Spirit to pray about that. Your prayer doesn't have to be long. We are not talking about investing a lot of time. Really, it doesn't take much time to say, "Lord, please draw them to You. Let them see You and learn Your truth."

There are lots of hurting people out there, people who are searching everywhere for peace, for love, for satisfaction, for happiness, for a new thrill to top the last one, for a purpose to live. We know the only One who gives peace and who knows the reason for life—every life. Let's pray that those lost people find Him. Let's pray that He steps into their lives, draws them to Him, and blesses them with His saving grace. The next time we are tempted to "tsk, tsk, tsk" at someone's antics, let's pray for them instead. When we witness a troublesome event, let's pray for those involved and for God's intervention.

Plan of Action:

1. Begin to watch the news from a new perspective. Look for people who need prayer and then pray for them.
2. In your everyday life, keep your senses open to find who around you needs prayer. Then pray for them.

Prayer:

Father, please remind me to pray for hurting people that I see on the news and in my everyday life. Every time I find myself feeling disgusted with the actions of people, nudge me to pray for them. Lord, I know that if they don't know You, they are lost. Move me to pray for those whose names come before me that they find You, Your peace, Your gift of salvation in Christ. Thank You, Lord. I pray in Jesus' name. Amen.

TREES

Scripture Reading: Psalm 139:1-18

"You are the salt of the earth . . . . You are the light of the world"
(Matthew 5:13-14).

I live in a development where the landscapers have trimmed the grass to perfection, the bushes to perfection, and almost all of the trees to perfection. In contrast, there are the Hong Kong orchid trees. Their branches spread out in all different directions and lengths. Their branches look like my hair when I wake up in the morning. But in December, some very pretty pink orchids bloom on the trees, and they have such a heavenly scent. When my husband and I walk past them, we always congratulate God on the great job He did with those trees. I'm sure that makes Him smile. We get just a dim glimpse of when God created the world, and He "saw all that he had made, and it was very good" (Genesis 1:31).

There are also walnut trees in our development. They are not really very pretty. We come from Kansas where there are beautiful deciduous trees, but in Southern Florida, where we live, the deciduous trees are not pretty. They are spindly with very small leaves. However, in December those leaves begin to fall onto the sidewalks, and they make a beautiful mosaic of burgundies, tans, and browns. God brings beauty from even those trees.

Looking at the walnut tree and the Hong Kong orchid tree and smelling its aroma reminds me that like them, God created a very unique me. I am not like anyone else, and I am not supposed to be. His beauty reflects best in me when I am just being myself, the way He created me for His glory (Isaiah 43:7), letting His Holy Spirit shine through me. 2 Corinthians 2:15 reminds us "For we are to God the pleasing aroma of Christ among those who are being saved and those who are perishing." Don't you love that? I am the pleasing aroma of Christ. You are the pleasing aroma of Christ. We can't get much better than that.

Plan of Action:

1. Consider your unique features and characteristics. Thank God that He created you just exactly the way you are. The only changes that need to be made will be made by the Holy Spirit as He makes us more and more like Christ.

2. Look at those people around you. God created them too. Ask God to help you appreciate them as His creation. Pray that they, too, accept Christ as their Savior and that they allow the Holy Spirit to wash them with His Word.

Prayer:

Lord, You created me for Your glory. I ask that You remind me that I am perfect in Your eyes just the way I am and I don't have to be like anyone else, only like Christ. I want Your light to shine through me to draw people to You and help me to be salt in this world to make people thirst for You. Thank You for loving me. Thank You for creating me just as I am. I pray in Jesus' name. Amen.

UNCOMFORTABLE

Scripture Reading: Exodus 20:1-17

"Do your best to present yourself to God as one approved, a workman who does not need to be ashamed and who correctly handles the word of truth" (Timothy 2:15).

One of my good friends told me that she knew of several people in her church who were having extramarital affairs. She went to the pastor, who had been there over 15 years, and asked him to preach on the Ten Commandments. She explained that she knew of several people in the church, and at least one elder, who were having affairs, and she felt the church body needed to be reminded of God's Word in relation to that. The pastor's response was, "Oh no. I wouldn't want to make anyone uncomfortable!"

Sadly, I knew this pastor, and I was not surprised by his answer. I have heard of pastors who fear losing their jobs more than they fear God's judgment on how they lead their flock. One of the responsibilities for a preacher is to preach God's Word (1 Timothy 4:13). In order to do that, he needs to spend time in the Word, asking the Holy Spirit to teach him and enable him to relay the messages to his congregation. The Apostle Paul asks in Romans 10:14-15, "How, then, can they call on the one they have not believed in? And how can they believe in the one of whom they have not heard? And how can they hear without someone preaching to them?" He also instructed Timothy, who served as a pastor, to make every effort to behave in a way that he would have no reason to be ashamed before God as to how he handled God's Word (2 Timothy 2:15-16).

Granted most people know what the Ten Commandments are, just like most people know that adultery is wrong. But there is something very convicting about hearing God's Word spoken and preached. How many of us have sat in church hearing a message from the pastor just knowing that even if the message was meant for no one else in the congregation, it was directed at us. Sometimes the message is uplifting and encouraging, and sometimes it is convicting and uncomfortable. Yes, we all know that sometimes God has to make us uncomfortable because we are continuing in behavior that doesn't honor Him and He wants us to change. "For the word of God is living and active. Sharper than any double-edged sword . . . ; it judges the thoughts and attitudes of the heart" (Hebrews 4:12). Using God's Word, the Holy Spirit points the supernatural laser directly to the sin that is hidden sometimes to the rest of the world and convicts us to deal with it.

We need to hear the Word of God on a regular basis, just as we need to study His Word regularly. ". . . Christ loved the church and gave himself up for her to make her holy, cleansing her by the washing with water through the word, . . . " (Ephesians 5:25-26). As we hear and study the Word, we are cleansed supernaturally. As we learn His Truth, He changes us to become more like Christ. Amazing.

Plan of Action:

1. Pray that your pastor takes his responsibility very seriously by spending time studying God's Word, preaching it with boldness, sitting before Him in prayer for his congregation. It doesn't hurt to pray that he is also interesting. ☺

2. Remember to pray for his family too.

3. Take your Bible to church or download a Bible App to your phone. Then when the Word is read, follow along to verify the accuracy of the reading.

Prayer:

Father, thank You for Your Word. Thank You for our pastors who have accepted Your call to lead a congregation. Please help them to listen to You and honor You in whatever they do. Give them courage to preach Your message every time they stand before their congregation, even if it might make someone uncomfortable. Bless them and protect them and their families. Help us to remember to encourage them periodically and let them know we appreciate them. And please, Lord, give us ears to hear Your messages. Thank You! In Jesus' name I pray. Amen.

ZACCHAEUS

Scripture Reading: Luke 19:1-10

"When Jesus reached the spot, he looked up and said to him, 'Zacchaeus, come down immediately. I must stay at your house today'" (Luke 19:5).

Zacchaeus was short and knew he wouldn't be able to see Jesus because of the crowd, and "[h]e wanted to see who Jesus was" (Luke 19:3). Thus, he climbed a sycamore tree ahead of the time that Jesus was passing through Jericho. Jesus knew he was there, singled him out, and told him to come down because He "must stay at your house today" (Luke 19:5). I read somewhere that this was the only time on record when the Savior invited Himself to someone's home. Then we read in Luke 19:6: "So he hurried and came down and received Him joyfully" (ESV). That makes me smile. Zacchaeus had gone hoping just to see Jesus, and he ends up with Jesus visiting his home.

Just as Jesus knew Zacchaeus was there among the crowd of people, so does Jesus know where you are all of the time every day. "You know when I sit and when I rise; you perceive my thoughts from afar. You discern my going out and my lying down; you are familiar with all my ways. Before a word is on my tongue you know it completely, O LORD. You hem me in—behind and before; you have laid your hand upon me" (Psalm 139:2-5). I love verse 5 from the *New Living Translation* of the Bible. "You go before me and follow me. You place your hand of blessing on my head." Isn't that a wonderful promise? He goes before us and follows us, and places

His hand of blessing on our heads. What a privileged people we are who know Christ as Savior and Lord!

Verse 2 of Luke 19 tells us that Zacchaeus was a tax collector, and in that time they had the reputation of being dishonest. Notice his reaction in verse 8 after just being in Jesus' presence. "Look Lord! Here and now I give half of my possessions to the poor, and if I have cheated anybody out of anything, I will pay back four times the amount." Just being in Christ's presence affects everyone. He is God in the flesh of man. Those who love Him are awed at His peace and love. They may also be convicted of some wrong that is in their life. They may be led to confess and make it right, as Zacchaeus did. Our loving Lord always forgives our wrongs, our sins. "If we confess our sins, he is faithful and just to forgive us our sins and to cleanse us from all unrighteousness" (1 John 1:9 ESV).

"For the Son of Man came to seek and to save what was lost" (Luke 19:10). Jesus sought out Zacchaeus, just as He sought you. Praise God for His wonderful gifts of grace and favor.

Plan of Action:

1. Take a few minutes and soak in the fact that Jesus knows you and even seeks you out. The Creator of the universe loves you and wants to "come to your house today."

2. Now I want you to imagine what you would do if Christ were physically coming to your house. Before you panic into thinking of all of the housework you feel that you need to do, remember the story in Luke 10:38-42 of Mary and Martha. Martha was distracted with preparations. Jesus said that Mary had chosen the better thing, and that was sitting at Jesus' feet to learn and worship Him. Therefore, what would you ask Him?

Prayer:

Lord, what a wonder You are! You love me so much that You died in my place to pay for my sin. I am in awe that You care about me. Thank You for my life. I am Yours, Lord. Take me and use me. Let me be an obedient servant, joyfully following every step You put before me. I love You, Lord. In Jesus' name. Amen.

APPENDIX I

Steps to Salvation with Scriptures

Romans 3:23 "All have sinned and fall short of the glory of God."

Romans 5:8 "But God demonstrates his own love for us in this: While we were still sinners, Christ died for us."

I John 1:9 "If we confess our sins, he is faithful and just and will forgive us our sins and purify us from all unrighteousness."

John 3:16 "For God so loved the world that he gave his one and only Son, that whoever believes in him shall not perish but have eternal life."

Romans 10:9 "If you confess with your mouth, 'Jesus is Lord,' and believe in your heart that God raised him from the dead, you will be saved."

John 1:12 "Yet to all who received him, to those who believed in his name, he gave the right to become children of God."

Philippians 1:6 "Being confident of this, that he who began a good work in you will carry it on to completion until the day of Christ Jesus."

3 Questions to Ask When Introducing Someone to Christ

These are taken from Leith Samuel from Southampton, England, and are quoted and expounded upon in Paul E. Little's book *How to Give Away Your Faith* (published by Intervarsity Press, Downers Grove, IL 1966 and 1988) on pages 84 and 85.

1. "Have you ever personally trusted Jesus Christ, or are you still on the way?"
   Then you listen to the person's answer.

2. "That's interesting. How far along the way are you?"
   Be hypersensitive to the condition of the person with whom you are speaking. This is the time when they may bring up the faith of their

grandmother, or how the Lord has been leading them lately, or any number of things, which may seem out of context. Listen, and ask the Holy Spirit to guide you along.

3. "Would you like to become a real Christian and be sure of it?"
   This would be a good time to take them through the scriptures above.

APPENDIX II

Step-by-Step Scriptures

He guides me in paths of righteousness for his name's sake.

(Psalm 23:3b)

Show me your ways, O Lord, teach me your paths. Guide me in your truth and teach me, for you are God my Savior, and my hope is in you all day long.

(Psalm 25:4-5)

Show me the path where I should go, O Lord; point out the right road for me to walk. Lead me; teach me; for you are the God who gives me salvation. I have no hope except in you.

(Psalm 25:4-5 TLB)

He guides the humble in what is right and teaches them his way.

(Psalm 25:9)

The Lord is good and glad to teach the proper path to all who go astray; he will teach the ways that are right and best to those who humbly turn to him. And when we obey him, every path he guides us on is fragrant with his loving-kindness and his truth.

(Psalms 25:8-10 TLB)

I will instruct you and teach you in the way you should go; I will counsel you and watch over you.

(Psalm 32:8)

I will instruct you (says the Lord) and guide you along the best pathway for your life; I will advise you and watch your progress.
(Psalm 32:8 TLB)

Taste and see that the Lord is good; blessed is the man who takes refuge in him . . . The lions may grow weak and hungry, but those who seek the Lord lack no good thing.
(Psalm 34:8, 10)

If the Lord delights in a man's way, he makes his steps firm; though he stumble, he will not fall, for the Lord upholds him with his hand.
(Psalm 37:23-24)

The steps of good men are directed by the Lord. He delights in each step they take.
(Psalm 37:23 TLB)

For this God is our God for ever and ever; he will be our guide even to the end.
(Psalm 48:14)

In God I trust; I will not be afraid, what can man do to me? . . . For you have delivered me from death and my feet from stumbling, that I may walk before God in the light of life.
(Psalm 56:11, 13)

Let everyone bless God and sing his praises, for he holds our lives in his hands. And he holds our feet to the path.
(Psalm 66:8-9 TLB)

Blessed are those whose strength is in you, who have set their hearts on pilgrimage . . . They go from strength to strength, till each appears before God in Zion.
(Psalm 84:5, 7)

APPENDIX II

Happy are those who are strong in the Lord, who want above all else to follow your steps . . . They will grow constantly in strength, and each of them is invited to meet with the Lord in Zion.

(Psalm 84:5, 7 TLB)

Teach me your way, O Lord, and I will walk in your truth; give me an undivided heart that I may fear your name.

(Psalm 86:11)

Tell me where you want me to go and I will go there. May every fiber of my being unite in reverence to your name.

(Psalm 86:11 TLB)

The Lord will keep you from all harm—he will watch over your life; the Lord will watch over your coming and going both now and forevermore.

(Psalm 121:7-8)

He keeps you from all evil, and preserves your life. He keeps his eye upon you as you come and go and always guards you.

(Psalm 121:7-8 TLB)

You hem me in—behind and before; and you have laid your hand upon me.

(Psalm 139:5)

You both precede and follow me and place your hand of blessing on my head.

(Psalm 139:5 TLB)

Let the morning bring me word of your unfailing love, for I have put my trust in you. Show me the way I should go, for to you I lift up my soul.

(Psalm 143:8)

Let me see your kindness to me in the morning, for I am trusting you. Show me where to walk, for my prayer is sincere.
(Psalm 143:8 TLB)

In his heart a man plans his course, but the Lord determines his steps.
(Proverbs 16:9)

We should make plans—counting on God to direct us.
(Proverbs 16:9 TLB)

A man's steps are directed by the Lord . . .
(Proverbs 20:24)

But they that wait upon the Lord shall renew their strength. They shall mount up with wings like eagles; they shall run and not be weary; they shall walk and not faint.
(Isaiah 40:31 TLB)

Fear not, for I am with you. Do not be dismayed. I am your God. I will strengthen you; I will help you; I will uphold you with my victorious right hand.
(Isaiah 41:10 TLB)

The Lord will guide you always; he will satisfy your needs in a sun-scorched land and will strengthen your frame. You will be like a well-watered garden, like a spring whose waters never fail.
(Isaiah 58:11)

I know, O Lord, that a man's life is not his own; it is not for man to direct his steps.
(Jeremiah 10:23)

When Jesus spoke again to the people, he said, "I am the light of the world. Whoever follows me will never walk in darkness, but will have the light of life."
(John 8:12)

Jesus answered, "I am the way and the truth and the life. No one comes to the Father except through me."

(John 14:6)

Faith comes from hearing the message, and the message is heard through the word of Christ.

(Romans 10:17)

No temptation has seized you except what is common to man. And God is faithful; he will not let you be tempted beyond what you can bear. But when you are tempted, he will also provide a way out so that you can stand up under it.

(1 Corinthians 10:13)

Since we live by the Spirit, let us keep in step with the Spirit.

(Galatians 5:25)

If any of you lacks wisdom, he should ask God, who gives generously to all without finding fault, and it will be given to him.

(James 1:5)

But if we walk in the light, as he is in the light, we have fellowship with one another, and the blood of Jesus, his Son, purifies us from all sin.

(1 John 1:7)

It has given me great joy to find some of your children walking in the truth, just as the Father commanded us.

(2 John 4)

APPENDIX III

Scriptures Referenced in the Devotional, excluding the Appendixes

Scripture Reference—*Devotion*

Genesis

1:31—*Trees*
2:16-17—*Fear Not*
3—*Fear Not*
9:12-17—*Remembering*
37—*Parents' Love for Their Children*

Exodus

2:23-25—*Remembering*
13:1-18—*GPS (Global Positioning System)*
15:20—*Sitting on the Outside, . . .*
20:1-17—*Uncomfortable*
33:15—*Comfortable; Depart, Depart*
34:29-35—*Reflect Him*

Numbers

13:26-14:35—*GPS (Global Positioning System)*

Deuteronomy

6:12—*Remembering*
6:10-12—*Boasting*
6:20-25—*Remembering*
8:1-18—*Remembering*
8:18—*Say "Thank You"*
31:8—*Fear Not*
32:7—*Remembering*

Joshua

1:5—*Depart, Depart; Nehemiah, Part 4, His Work Is Challenged*
1:9—*Say "Thank You"*

1 Samuel

3:1-10—*Invisible*

2 Samuel

6:14—*Sitting on the Outside, . . .*

1 Kings

1:1-53—*Leaders*

Nehemiah

1-2:8—*Nehemiah, Part 1, Fasts and Prays*
2:11-18—*Nehemiah, Part 3, Prepares and Presents*
2:8-20—*Nehemiah, Part 2, Experiences Opposition*
2:20—*Depart, Depart*
2:19-20—*Nehemiah, Part 4, His Work Is Challenged*
4:1-23—*Nehemiah, Part 2, Experiences Opposition; Nehemiah, Part 4, His Work Is Challenged*
6:1-4—*Nehemiah, Part 4, His Work Is Challenged*
6:10-13—*Nehemiah, Part 4, His Work Is Challenged*
6:15-16—*Nehemiah, Part 4, His Work Is Challenged*
9:6—*Coincidence*

Job

14:5—*Fear Not*
38-39—*Coincidence*

Psalms

1:1-3—*Ants*
10:17—*Say "Thank You"*
12:8—*GPS (Global Positioning System)*
14:2-3—*Righteous*
16:5-11—*Glorify God*
19—*Let Us Be Salty . . .*
19:7—*God's Work in Us*
23—*Plans*
25:4-5—*God's Guidance*
25:9—*Pride and Humility*
27:2-4—*Adventures*
31:24—*Say "Thank You"*
32:8—*Depart, Depart; God's Guidance; His Sovereignty; Just Turn the Page*
41:1—*Misplaced Expectations*
46:9-11—*Coincidence*
68:15-16—*His Sovereignty*
71—*His Sovereignty*
75:6—*Change of Leadership*
75:6-7—*Leaders*
95:6-7—*The Good Shepherd*
96:11-12—*Praise the Lord*
98:8—*Praise the Lord*
100—*Grace Extenders*
100:3—*The Good Shepherd*
101:3a—*Fear Not*
103:12—*Righteous*
111—*Praise the Lord*

APPENDIX III

112—*Praise the Lord*
113—*Praise the Lord*
119:11—*Adventures; Suggestions for Using This Devotional*
119:18—*Ants; Adventures*
119:96-97—*Adventures*
119:105—*Our Home Churches*
119:98—*God's Work in Us*
121—*God's Guidance*
121:1-2—*Say "Thank You"*
127:3—*Parents' Love for Their Children*
133:1—*Division in the Body*
136—*His Love Endures Forever*
138—*Praise the Lord*
138:7-8—*Fear Not*
139:5—*Nehemiah, Part 2: Experiences Opposition; Fear Not; Just Turn the Page*
139:2-3—*Coincidence*
139:2-5—*Zacchaeus*
139:6—*Prayers*
139:7-12—*Coincidence*
139:13—*Boasting; Depart, Depart*
139:1-18—*Adventures; Parents' Love for Their Children; Trees*
139:1-18, 23-24—*GPS (Global Positioning System)*
139:23-24—*Grace Extenders*
143—*Depart, Depart*
144-150—*Praise the Lord*
145:9—*Souvenirs*
145:9-10a—*Praise the Lord*
148—*Praise the Lord*
149:3—*Sitiing on the Outside, . . .*
150—*Sitting on the Outside, . . .*

Proverbs

3:5-6—*GPS (Global Positioning System)*
4:18—*Let Us Be Salty Salt . . .*
16:1—*Plans*
19:21—*Leaders*
21:1—*Nehemiah, Part 2, Experiences Opposition*
31:30—*God's Work in Us*

Ecclesiastes

3:1—*Ants; Nehemiah, Part 3, Prepares and Presents*
3:7b—*Nehemiah, Part 3, Prepares and Presents*
4:9-12—*Souvenirs*

Isaiah

6:5—*Our Speech*
41:10—*Fear Not*
42:5-6a—*Say "Thank You"*
43:2-3—*Adventures*
43:4—*Gloify God*
43:7—*Trees*
46:9—*Prayers*
46:9b-11—*Coincidence*
48:17—*Depart, Depart; GPS (Global Positioning System); His Sovereignty; Prayers*
49:15-16—*Remembering*
49:16—*Nehemiah, Part 2, Experiences Opposition*
52:11-12—*Depart, Depart*
54:10—*His Love Endures Forever*
55:11—*Admittance*
61:1-3—*Misplaced Expectations*

Jeremiah

9:23-24—*Boasting*
10:23—*God's Guidance*
29:13—*Confirm Your Facts*
32:17—*Prayers*
33:3—*God's Guidance; His Sovereignty*

Ezekiel

37:1-14—*Our Home Churches*

Jonah

1-4—*Just Turn the Page*

Zephaniah

3:17—*His Love Endures Forever*

Matthew

5:6—*Righteous*
7:7-11—*Prayers*
5:9—*Change of Leadership*
5:10-12—*Persecution*
5:13-14—*Trees*
5:13-16—*Let Us Be Salty . . .*
6:33—*Righteous*
7:7—*Confirm Your Facts; The Blind Man*
7:7-8—*Confirm Your Facts; Misplaced Expectations; Our Home Churches*
7:11—*Prayers*
7:20—*A Sure Foundation*
7:24-27—*A Sure Foundation*
9:37—*Nehemiah, Part 4, His Work Is Challenged*
10:29—*Coincidence*
10:30—*Coincidence; Comfortable*
21:22—*The Blind Man*
22:39—*Coincidence*
28:18-20—*Division in the Body*
28:19—*Nehemiah, Part 4, His Work Is Challenged*
28:19-20—*His Love Endures Forever*

Mark

5:1-20—*Let Us Be Salty Salt . . .*
5:25-34—*Let Us Be Salty Salt . . .*
10:46—*The Blind Man*
12:28-31—*Aunt Merle*
16:6—*Righteous*
16:15—*Admittance*

Luke

1:37—*His Love Endures Forever*
1:41-44—*Confirm Your Facts*
2:8-20—*The Good Shepherd*
2:21-35—*Simeon*
7:11-28—*Confirm Your Facts*
8:26-39—*Have You Told Anyone Lately?*
9:46-48—*Aunt Merle*
10:25-37—*The Good Samaritan*
10:38-42—*Ants; Zacchaeus*
11:13—*Simeon*
11:9-13—*Take the Headlines . . .*
14:13-14—*The Blind Man*
17:11-19—*Say "Thank You"*
18:35-43—*The Blind Man*
19:1-10—*Zacchaeus*
19:40—*Praise the Lord*

John

1:12—*Righteous*
2:1—*Our Speech*
3:16—*Fear Not; GPS (Global Positioning System); His Love Endures Forever; Souvenirs*
4:7-42—*Let Us Be Salty Salt . . .*
6:44—*Grace Extenders*
7:37b—*Let Us Be Salty Salt . . .*
10:7-18—*Admittance*
10:1-30—*The Good Shepherd*
10:15—*Our Place in Heaven*
13:34—*Aunt Merle; Our Home Churches*
14:1-4—*Our Place in Heaven*
14:6—*The Good Shepherd; Righteous; Admittance*
14:13-14—*The Blind Man*
14:15-31—*The Breeze*
14:26—*Adventures; Remembering*
15:1-8—*Butterflies and Other Personalities*
15:5—*God's Work in Us*
15:16—*God's Work in Us*

Acts

2:38—*Simeon*
2:42-47—*Entertaining Strangers*
4:13—*God's Work in Us*
9:1-10—*Comfortable*
10:9-16—*Comfortable; Just Turn the Page*
10:28—*Comfortable; Just Turn the Page*
10-11:35—*Coincidence*
17:25—*Say "Thank You"*
17:26—*Our Home Churches*
22—*Comfortable*
26—*Comfortable*
26:9-11—*Comfortable*

Romans

3:1—*Leaders*
3:23—*Change of Leadership; Division in the Body; Pride and Humility; Righteous*
5:8—*Our Speech; Righteous*
6:23—*Righteous*
8:28—*Prayers*
8:28-30—*God's Work in Us*
8:34—*Righteous*
8:38-39—*Coincidence*
10:13—*Zacchaeus*
10:14-15—*Uncomfortable*
11:11-24—*His Love Endures Forever*
11:13-24—*Misplaced Expectations*
12:2—*God's Work in Us*
12:3—*Butterflies and Other Personalities*

1 Corinthians

1:31—*Boasting*
6:8-9—*Our Speech*
10:31—*Butterflies and Other Personalities; Glorify God; Our Speech*
11:23b-26—*Remembering*
12:12-27—*Division in the Body*
14:20—*Fear Not*
15:58—*Group Dynamics*

2 Corinthians

1:21-22—Grace Extenders
2:14-15—Butterflies and Other Personalities
2:15—Trees
3:18—God's Work in Us; Groups Dynamics; Reflect Him
5:17-21—Group Dynamics
5:20—Nehemiah, Part 4, His Work Is Challenged; Persecution
5:21—Righteous; Simeon
6:18—Fear Not
9:8—Grace Extenders
11:24-32—Persecution

Galatians

5:22-23—Butterflies and Other Personalities; Glorify God; Persecution
5:25-26—Division in the Body
6:10—Butterflies and Other Personalities; Division in the Body

Ephesians

1:1-14—Chosen
1:4-6—The Good Shepherd
1:5—His Love Endures Forever
2:8-9—Boasting; God's Work in Us; Grace Extenders; Righteous; A Sure Foundation
2:10—Righteous
2:1-10—Misplaced Expectations
2:20—God's Work in Us
3:6—Coincidence
3:12—The Blind Man
3:20-21—But God
4:2—Boasting
4:13—Grace Extenders
4:29—Say "Thank You"
4:29-31—Division in the Body
5:1-17—Our Speech
5:25-26—Uncomfortable
5:26—Butterflies and Other Personalities

Philippians

1:6—God's Work in Us; Righteous; Suggestions for Using This Devotional
2:3—Butterflies and Other Personalities; Division in the Body
2:3-11—The "Right" Way
2:5-7—The "Right" Way
2:5-8—Pride and Humility
2:13—Just Turn the Page
2:14-15—The "Right" Way
3:21—God's Work in Us
4:4-8—But God
4:6—Take the Headlines . . .
4:6-7—Leaders
4:8—Fear Not
4:11b—Comfortable
4:19—But God; Parents' Love for Their Children

Colossians

1:12—God's Work in Us
1:16—Souvenirs
3:12—Entertaining Strangers

APPENDIX III

3:16—*Adventures*
3:17—*Let Us Be Salty Salt . . . ; Say "Thank You"*
3:23-24—*Change of Leadership*
4:3-4—*His Love Endures Forever*
4:6—*Let Us Be Salty Salt . . .*

1 Thessalonians

5:11—*Butterflies and Other Personalities; Say "Thank You"*
5:16—*Nehemiah, Part 1, Fasts and Prays*
5:16-18—*Invisible*
5:17—*A Sure Foundation*

1 Timothy

1:15—*Boasting*
2:1—*Take the Headlines . . .*
2:1-2—*Leaders*
4:13—*Uncomfortable*
5:10—*Aunt Merle*

2 Timothy

2:15—*Suggestions for Using This Devotional*
2:15-16—*Uncomfortable*
3:16-17—*Adventures; Just Turn the Page*

Titus

3:1-2—*Change of Leadership*
3:4-5—*Righteous*
3:5—*God's Work in Us*

Hebrews

4:2—*Suggestions for Using This Devotional*
4:12—*Adventures; Uncomfortable*
10:24-25—*Say "Thank You"*
13:1-2—*Entertaining Strangers*
13:8—*Have You Told Anyone Lately?; Just Turn the Page*
13:20-21—*Suggestions for Using This Devotional*

James

1:5—*God's Guidance; Misplaced Expectations*
1:17—*Prayers*
4:2—*The Blind Man*
4:7-8—*Our Speech*
5:9—*Butterflies and Other Personalities*
5:16—*Righteous*

1 Peter

1:3-4
3:12—*Righteous*
4:8-10—*Souvenirs*
4:8-11—*Aunt Merle*
4:9—*Butterflies and Other Personalities*
5:7—*Fear Not; Misplaced Expectations*

2Peter

3:9b—*Group Dynamics*

1 John
1:9—*Zacchaeus*
1:7-10—*Righteous*
2:1—*Righteous*
3:8—*Division in the Body*

Jude
16—*Butterflies and Other Personalities*

ONE LAST NOTE FROM THE AUTHOR

My Dear Reader,

If you have been blessed while reading this devotional, you may want to get my first book: *Lord, It's Time for Just You and Me.* You may email me at clynnbetz@gmail.com to order it.

Or you may want to buy my second book: *Lord, It's Time for Just You and Me, Book 2*, which you can find at www.amazon.com.

I do pray that God has used your reading of *Lord, It's Time for Just You and Me, Book 3* to draw you closer to Him. Let's glorify Him and enjoy Him together!

Blessings and Love in Christ,
Cheryl Lynn Betz

www.ingramcontent.com/pod-product-compliance
Lightning Source LLC
Chambersburg PA
CBHW080449170426
43196CB00016B/2734